Games with a Purpose

Previous books by Martin Saunders:
The Ideas Factory
The Think Tank
Youth Work from Scratch
The Beautiful Disciplines
500 Prayers for Young People

GAMES
WITH A PURPOSE

200 icebreakers, energizers,
and games that make a point

Martin Saunders
and Jimmy Young

MONARCH
BOOKS

Published by Monarch Books
an imprint of
Lion Hudson plc
Wilkinson House, Jordan Hill Road,
Oxford OX2 8DR, England
Email: monarch@lionhudson.com
www.lionhudson.com/monarch

ISBN 978 0 85721 559 8
e-ISBN 978 0 85721 560 4

First edition 2016

Acknowledgements
Scripture quotations taken from the Holy Bible, New International Version
Anglicised. Copyright © 1979, 1984, 2011 Biblica, formerly International
Bible Society. Used by permission of Hodder & Stoughton Ltd, an Hachette
UK company. All rights reserved. "NIV" is a registered trademark of Biblica.
UK trademark number 1448790; The Holy Bible, English Standard Version®
(ESV®) copyright © 2001 by Crossway, a publishing ministry of Good News
Publishers. All rights reserved; The Holy Bible: International Standard Version.
Release 2.0, Build 2015.02.09. Copyright © 1995-2014 by ISV Foundation. ALL
RIGHTS RESERVED INTERNATIONALLY; the New American Standard Bible®,
Copyright © 1960, 1962, 1963, 1968, 1971, 1972, 1973, 1975, 1977, 1995 by
The Lockman Foundation. Used by permission; The Authorized (King James)
Version. Rights in the Authorized Version are vested in the Crown. Reproduced
by permission of the Crown's patentee, Cambridge University Press.

A catalogue record for this book is available from the British Library

Contents

Acknowledgments

We'd like to thank our ever-patient wives, Jo and Debs; also Sally, the very kind lady in Crawley Starbucks who told us about the free refills; and the hundreds of unsuspecting young people who've been our game-invention guinea pigs over the years. Most of all, though, Martin would like to thank Tony Collins and Jenny Muscat at Monarch for demonstrating more patience in waiting for the manuscript than Doctor Who did in that episode where he gets stuck in the same place for several billion years. Martin is sorry.

Introduction

This is not a book of games.

Well, all right, strictly speaking it is. The game-based title on the cover, the list of different types of games on the contents page, and the fact that the cursory glance you took through the book when you first picked it up revealed pages and pages of games... they're all dead giveaways.

So let me try again: this is not *just* a book of games.

There have been plenty of great youth ministry games compendiums in the past. J. Arthur Johnson's seminal *400 Ice-Breakers to Warm Them Up* (Blandington Press, 1969) is probably the first example, while Lee, Ingleton, Ellis, and Sedgwick's *3,000 Great Youth Group Games* (Know Hope Books, 1981, now sadly out of print) is unrivalled in terms of sheer scale. But what all of these books have in common is an obsessive focus on games and games alone. They never set their ice-breakers, energizers, or other fun activities in the context of the wider youth group session.

This book starts from a slightly different place. We've all been there – trying to plan an interesting, thought-provoking session for young people. We have a subject; we may also have a specific Bible passage that we're going to address with them. Every element of the session is carefully woven together to help our group to engage fully with the subject; to go on a journey of learning, discussion, and discovery.

Yet we're also conscious of the need to make the gathering enjoyable. We need to put a game or two in there, in order to expend a bit of energy (or bring energy into the room), put a smile on their faces, and help make the session as a whole more memorable. So we stare at the blank sheet of paper/iPad screen/Post-it Note in front of us. We think, and think, and think some more. And then we write those two words down once again: "Chubby Bunnies".[1]

---

1   DISCLAIMER: Of course, I'm only joking. No one plays that game any more – it's dangerous and very inappropriate. It was just the obvious punchline.

The problem is that – speaking from personal experience – it's often very difficult to find the right game for the right youth session. We play games because they're fun, not because they're part of the overall journey of the meeting. This book is an effort to address that disconnect – to provide you with games which link in with whatever subject or theme you're addressing in your session. It's a book of games with a purpose – the purpose being to drive your gathering of young people forward in a way that's meaningful, not random.

So this is a book of games, but it's not *just* a book of games.

At this point, it seems like a good idea to introduce myself. I'm Martin, and I've been involved in running youth groups in a Christian faith context for close to fifteen years at time of writing. I've worked in churches where the youth group has been 150-strong and met in a huge multi-purpose venue; I've set up groups from scratch with four young people meeting in a living room. In both of those settings, and most places in between, I've had to plan and run games, and watch them either flourish or flag hopelessly. Hopefully this experience has equipped me well for the journey we're about to take together.

I also previously edited the British magazine *Youthwork* for almost a decade. As part of that magazine's monthly resource supplement, it was my job to equip youth leaders with ready-to-use games which they could easily adapt and use in their work with young people. And it's at this point that I should also introduce my co-writer.

Jimmy was my go-to games man throughout my time at *Youthwork* magazine. A seasoned youth worker, Jimmy had developed a legendary list of tried and tested games to use with teenagers. So when it came to creating a book of Games with a Purpose, there was only one man to call.

From here on in, the introductory sections of the book will be written in a conversation between two font styles. Since I went first, I get to write in standard text like this. Since he's now left full-time youth work and been ordained, Jimmy will take the humble path of italics. Say hello Jimmy.

Hello Jimmy.

You can see immediately how much fun he is.

*Wait. I didn't say that. I'm sitting opposite you, and you typed that. That's not my voice. **This** is my voice.*

(Although on the written page it is admittedly difficult to prove that).

And I am indeed humble. Humble enough to admit that pretty much all the games in this book have been tried, tested, and/or created by an army of youth workers across the world. We are simply the... er... conduit?... medium? ... people? (yes, definitely, we are people) who have managed to gather these things together. So hello.

You have of course purchased/been passed/illegally photocopied[2] this book because you are interested in the actual games themselves, so we promise not to drone on for too long in these introductory sections like two men with no social awareness. However, before we do plunge into the good stuff, please permit us to briefly share a little bit of the thinking behind this book, and to explain how we think you might make best use of it.

Why we play games

Young people love playing games. Doing so allows them to hold on to (or even recapture) a bit of their childhood, and as people who are attracted to fun, risk, and adventure, game-playing is as natural an activity for them as eating and falling asleep (both of which they also enjoy immensely).

It's not just about childlikeness, however; games are a huge part of youth culture. From the growth of the youth-led video-gaming industry (now more profitable than Hollywood) to the rise of "gamification" (where elements of game playing are applied to things like learning and marketing to make them more attractive), games are everywhere for young people. It makes total sense for them to encounter them in a youth group context.

And, of course, they're fun! I'm a big believer in Fun: not the indie band, pop-pickers, but the idea of enjoying life. God isn't miserable, and doesn't want us to live in misery; we're called to life in all its fullness, and modelling that to our young people in the way we structure and create our sessions is so important.

2   I do hope not.

Perhaps the key word should be "joy"? Not simply "happy"or "cheery" – that way can lead to shallow engagement with the world, where it all becomes about what we can get out of it or how it makes us feel – but joy, that deeper sense of being. Some of the best youth group sessions I've been privileged to be involved in have been infused with a real sense of joy – where people simply enjoy sharing life and journeying together. And games are a great way of fostering that spirit.

Beyond that though, we also believe that games are a great way in to the deeper stuff (not that joy can't be deep). Not only do they relax young people (and their leaders), and reduce inhibitions, but they can also be used to introduce a theme or part of the Bible. So instead of just running a random game before your in-depth study on Daniel in the Lions' Den, you could precede it with a round of sleeping lions (terrible idea, sorry) or by unleashing a live lion on the group as a sort of high-octane chase game (not really). That's really the premise of this book in a nutshell (not the bit about the lions). Instead of simply playing games in our youth work, we can be playing relevant games which help to build a continuity of subject in our sessions. That's the "purpose" described in our title: to use fun and games to introduce themes and ideas to young people.

How to use this book

We're not going to insult your intelligence (*although we might at times insult one another's*); this is obviously a book of games, and you know how to use it.

While we've specified minimum suggested ages, this is a guide, and many of them may also work well with older groups.

You should also be aware of any safety issues involved in running these games, especially if they involve food and could trigger allergies among some young people. In addition, we'd like to make just a few simple suggestions to guide you on your way:

1. Don't use it as an excuse not to plan...

The best youth sessions are almost always the best-planned ones (and don't let the rogue exceptions to that rule fool you). So don't use this or any other resource as a total substitute for sitting down, praying, and putting together the best session you can.

2. Adapt the games for your group

The games are good (if we do say so ourselves), but they can be even better if you adapt them to the specific needs of your group. If you work in a place where you can be outside easily (let's say you do youth work in Honolulu[3]) then see if you can't slightly alter the versions of the games we've given you to make them work outside the context of the cold and draughty church halls we pictured as we wrote them. Or if there are ideas which you think won't quite work with your too-cool-for-school teens, then feel free to change them for something else. This book is a better resource when you invest it with your own ideas.

3. Consider pairing this resource with another

This book only gives you one element of your youth session, but there are plenty of other resources around which would work well as a companion. My books *The Ideas Factory* and *The Think Tank* (also Monarch) each contain 100 faith-based discussion starters, many of which link with the themes or "purposes" of these games. Lots of other great resources are available too – including Urban Saints' Energize materials, the meeting guides found in *Youthwork*, and various books published by Group/Simply Youth Ministry in the United States.

We hope that this book will be genuinely helpful in both providing you with great games for youth ministry, and helping your youth work meetings to be more coherent and theme-based. Most of all though, we hope that you and your young people have an amazing amount of fun.

Let the games commence!

---

3   If your job becomes available at any point, please do let us know.

1

Ice-Breakers

Parties. You either love them or you hate them. But however you feel, even the most extreme extroverts can struggle with the horror of realizing that they've walked into a social situation where they don't know a single other person. And without the help of a skilled host, many hours of painful small talk and floor-staring can often ensue as a result.

> *I kill at small talk. I can talk about weather, or motorway routes, or anything at all and nothing in particular for hours and hours... It's a particularly useful Church of England skill:*
>
> *"Yes, Mrs Jones, it has been unseasonably mild this last week, hasn't it?... And how are your begonias?" (I actually wouldn't know a begonia if I saw one, but I've definitely had a conversation about them on more than one occasion.)*

Youth groups can be a little bit like this, especially when some or all of the group are unfamiliar with each other. Most youth workers will recognize the awkwardly silent atmosphere of a new youth group, where every member has become suddenly intrigued by their own shoelaces. In these instances, the trusty youth group ice-breaker becomes an essential resource.

> *Or begonias. They're always good to have in reserve as a go-to. Or not. Ice-breaker games are probably more*

useful in this instance. Yes, actually; in the context of this book, let's stick with games.

The games in this chapter, then, are all designed for use in a context which might be described as a little icy. I'm not suggesting that they're best employed on a mountainside or in the depths of winter, but rather where the relational situation is in need of some thawing. These are games that inject a bit of life into a quiet room, which help young people to connect with one another, and lose their inhibitions a little. They include unfamiliar takes on familiar favourites, games which intentionally require young people to ask each other questions, and even one specifically aimed at those same introverts who always decline those party invitations. Hopefully, among them you'll find some resources which help your group members to feel a little more comfortable with one another.

1. Rock, Paper, Scissor mayhem!

Theme connection: Challenge, justice

Age suitability: 8+

Resources needed: Lots of simple paper "tokens" – enough for five per player, a small prize

Venue requirements: Enough space for the group to move around freely

Background preparation: None

The game

Give everyone in your group five tokens. Now invite them to walk around the room, playing rock, paper, scissors with as many people as they can. This is a very simple game involving three hand gestures; two opposing players produce one of these gestures at exactly the same moment. Remember:

- **Paper** (flat palm) covers rock (paper wins)

- **Rock** (fisted hand) blunts scissors (rock wins)

- **Scissors** (two fingers, split like scissors) cut paper (scissors wins)

If players produce the same gesture, they replay. Every time someone wins a game, they take one token from the loser.

Once each person is out of tokens, they sit down. After five minutes, get the remaining players to count their tokens and give a small prize to the person with the most.

What's the purpose?

Possible learning/discussion point from this game:

* The nature of our prevailing capitalist worldview is that over time a few people have ended up with most of the resources. There are "winners and losers" in this culture, but the problem is that the "losers" have no way of getting back into the game, because the "winners" have all the assets and resources.

2. Blindfolded charades

Theme connection: Listening to God, faith, discernment

Age suitability: 11+

Resources needed: Blindfold for every person attending, cue cards

Venue requirements: None, although a quiet venue is preferable

Background preparation: Write out cue cards containing some simple mime-able words or phrases, e.g. "Harry Potter", "Winnie the Pooh", "Facebook". You'll need to adapt these to the age/ability level of your group.

The game

Ask for two volunteers, and bring them out to the front. Now give everyone else apart from these two a blindfold and ask them to put it on.

Explain that you're going to play charades… with a difference. One of your volunteers is going to mime the phrase which you've written on a cue card but, of course, no one will be able to see the mime!

The other volunteer, then, is your interpreter. He or she must describe accurately what the first volunteer is miming, so that those listening can imagine the mime and begin to piece together the phrase. It's very important that the interpreter doesn't try to guess the answer themselves though – they just have to describe what they're seeing.

If it's not going very well, help things along a little. If it does work well, consider playing another round or two.

What's the purpose?

Possible learning/discussion points from this game:

- The Bible talks about the gift of "interpretation" (1 Corinthians 12:10) which complements other gifts like prophecy and speaking in tongues. Sometimes when God speaks, he provides an interpreter to help us understand him.

- The prophets in the Bible were people who "interpreted" God. This game provides a little picture of how their role worked – they explained what they thought God was saying to a people who couldn't otherwise hear him. But just as in this game, sometimes the prophets were still misunderstood…

3. Beach ball keepy-uppy

Theme connection: Teamwork

Age suitability: 9+

Resources needed: A beach ball (the larger the better)

Venue requirements: Enough space to kick/hit a ball around

Background preparation: None (apart from inflating the beach ball!)

The game

Using a beach ball, play the classic playground game of keepy-uppy, where the aim is to keep the ball off the ground for as long as possible using only your head and feet/legs. (If your group is prone to excessive displays of force, ban volleys and make it headers only as the beach ball may not have the necessary strength to survive a full-blown booting!) Count the number of times you've kept the ball off the ground if you want to make it competitive.

This also works well as a session opener while waiting for everyone to gather, as it can be played by any number from 2 to 100 (well, maybe not quite that many).

What's the purpose?

Possible learning/discussion points from this game:

- This can lead into a general discussion on teamwork.

- The lightness of the beach ball makes something which some people think is impossible less difficult; this is a great metaphor for some of the more apparently difficult elements of faith.

4. Scissor game

Theme connection: Challenge, communication

Age suitability: 9+

Resources needed: A pair of scissors

Venue requirements: None

Background preparation: None

The game

Get your group seated in a circle and explain that you are going to pass around a pair of scissors, and as you do so you need to state whether you pass them crossed or not. Pass the pair to the person sitting next to you and say "I pass you these scissors crossed/ uncrossed" (as appropriate), and then ask that person to pass them on and say whether they are crossed or not.

The secret twist is that whether the scissors can be described as crossed or not depends entirely on whether the legs of the person passing them on are crossed or not. Obviously, do not tell your group this! Instead, when it is your turn ostentatiously open/close the scissors, twist them round in your hands a number of times, or do whatever you like really with the scissors to bamboozle your group, before passing them on and announcing (correctly) whether you are passing them on crossed or not.

As the scissors are passed around make sure you comment on whether the passer's statement is correct. Your group will swiftly generate their own theories and rules as to how they are crossed or not, and it can be hilarious as their theories are shattered/strengthened by your correction or affirmation of the passer's statements. You can keep this going as long as you like, possibly returning to it later in the session, or in a future week, until the majority of the group have either worked it out or been driven mad by their failure to guess the rule!

What's the purpose?

Possible learning/discussion points from this game:

- Have you ever discovered that things are not as you expect them to be?

- When you pass things on to people, how can you be sure that they understand what you're trying to say?

5. The Toothbrush Game

Theme connection: Memory, identity

Age suitability: 7+

Resources needed: None

Venue requirements: None

Background preparation: None

The game

Get everyone sitting in a circle so you can all see each other, and introduce yourself by saying your name and the colour of your toothbrush. The person on your left then has to introduce themselves, saying their name and the colour of their toothbrush, as well as repeating your name and colour of toothbrush. The person on their left then has to do the same thing (name, colour of toothbrush plus the same information from everyone who has shared already) and proceed round the circle until the poor final person has to recite everyone's names plus the colour of their toothbrushes. (Perhaps as leader you can then demonstrate your great care and attention to detail by having another go yourself!)

There are any number of variations of this game – all you need to do is change the information they need to share, e.g. favourite food, colour, etc. – or if you want to secretly psychoanalyse your group ask them to come up with an adjective that describes themselves using the first letter of their name, e.g. Funny Frank, Deep Delilah, etc. (Be generous with the definition of adjective and/or spellings for those with names that don't lend themselves to adjectives – little Xavier or Zac might struggle!)

What's the purpose?

Possible learning/discussion points from this game:

- Do they think having a good memory is helpful or a hindrance? Why?

- Discovering our identity is a crucial part of childhood and the teenage years; working out what makes you "you", and whether that changes over time, is a big step in self-actualisation.

6. Memory Mingle

Theme connection: Memory, community

Age suitability: 11+

Resources needed: Post-it Notes, pens, paper

Venue requirements: Enough space for people to mill around

Background preparation: Write the names of various famous people on Post-it Notes – Lionel Messi, Barack Obama, Lady Gaga, and so on. Make a few of them a little more obscure; lesser known pop stars, actors, or sportspeople would work well.

The game

Ask your group to stand in a line. Walk along it and stick one Post-it to each of the young people's foreheads, without letting them see the name written on it. (It's worth saying at this point that this ISN'T the familiar game you're expecting…)

Before you send them off to circulate, explain that they have TWO objectives: a) to find out who they are by asking questions of the other players; b) to remember as many of the famous names they encounter as possible.

Send them off to mingle with each other for three minutes. At the end of this time, give each of them a pen and paper, and challenge them to write down as many of the names they can remember as possible.

They get a point for every name on their list, plus THREE points if they manage to include the name that was on their own head.

Ask them to be honest in scoring themselves, then award a small chocolate prize to the person with the most points.

What's the purpose?

Possible learning/discussion points from this game:

- Remembering important things can be a massive source of encouragement for Christians – in moments of doubt it's those memories of how God has worked in our lives that keep us going.

- It makes a massive difference to people when we remember their names – making them feel welcome and part of things. This is a really important skill to learn if you're going to be a welcoming community which attracts new people.

7. Common ground

Theme connection: Community, church

Age suitability: 11+

Resources needed: Chocolate bar big enough for two people to share, pens and paper (optional)

Venue requirements: None

Background preparation: None

The game

Ask the members of the group to pair up – specifically choosing someone that they don't know very well. If they're averse to the idea, explain that they probably have more chance of winning an amazing chocolate prize (size up to you) if they're not partnered with a close friend.

Now, give the pairs three to five minutes to talk with one another – and in that time to discover three surprising things which they have in common. The more unusual the connection, the better.

Possible common ground:

- Both like the same obscure band.

- Both visited the same tiny island.

- Both have a mum called Sandra.

- Both met the same celebrity.

(If they need help, explain that the trick is for one person to talk about lots of details of their life, with the other person chipping in when they find a link.)

After the time has elapsed, invite each pair to feed back to the group. Award the chocolate bar to the pair with the most bizarre or interesting connection.

What's the purpose?

Possible learning/discussion point from this game:

- Our group – and/or church – is made up of lots of very different people. God has created us all to be unique, and the experiences in our lives take us in lots of different directions. That said, there are also lots of things we have in common – passions, interests, and experiences we share – and that's often a building block of relationships.

8. Balloon Stomp

Theme connection: Wisdom, innocence

Age suitability: 9+

Resources needed: A plentiful supply of balloons (at least one per player), a ball of wool/string

Venue requirements: A large space to run around in

Background preparation: Inflate your balloons, and tie each one to a piece of wool/string with a simple loop at the end.

The game

Attach the balloons to the ankles of the young people – normally one per peson, although if you're extravagant and flush with balloons you could do one to each leg for more intense fun – and on your command allow them to attempt to pop each other's balloons by stamping on them. Once their balloon is popped the young people are "out" and retire to the sidelines. The winner is the last person to have an unpopped balloon.

A tip: make sure the balloons are fully inflated, as under-inflated balloons are tricky to pop. Also, the longer the string the more fun it is.

Additionally, if you're looking for a novel way of dividing your young people into groups, put a piece of paper with a number on it into each balloon before inflating. Get the young people to pick up their balloon detritus and number once they have popped, and get them into groups with others of the same number.

What's the purpose?

Possible learning/discussion points from this game:

- Jesus said we should be "wise as serpents, and as innocent as doves" (Matthew 10 v 16) – so how does that apply to this game (where you have to be sneaky to win), and more broadly to life?

- What's the best approach to this game – full-on attack, or hang around to try and sneakily pop other people's balloons? Does this connect to how we face other challenges?

9. Top box

Theme connection: Challenge

Age suitability: 7+

Resources needed: As many boxes as you have, a variety of objects to throw (e.g. a selection of balls of different sizes/weights, cushions, paper aeroplanes, cuddly toys – in other words, anything you have lying around!)

Venue requirements: Space to throw!

Background preparation: Set out the boxes around your room, and mark out a throwing line

The game

A very simple use for lots of boxes is to put things in them. And a fun way of doing this is doing so from a distance.

Get your young people to stand behind the lines and throw the objects into the boxes. Allocate each box different points for a successful throw and allow your young people chances to throw the objects into whichever target they choose. Keep a tally of who scores what, and make sure that everyone throws the same objects as each other overall.

What's the purpose?

Possible learning/discussion point from this game:

* Does setting/aiming for targets fill you with dread or a sense of purpose?

10. The Name Game

Theme connection: Identity, community

Age suitability: 9+

Resources needed: Paper, pens, "hat"

Venue requirements: None

Background preparation: None

The game

Give your players each a dozen or so pieces of paper (you can do as many as you like really, the more the better). Get them to write down names of famous people (you can offer certain guidelines if you wish, e.g. TV stars, Bible characters, sportspeople – but they do need to be known to the group, so no "my cousin Bob from Hull"). Once they've written the names, get them to fold their bits of paper and put them all into a hat or suitable alternative.

Divide everybody into two teams and explain that the game involves guessing the names on the pieces of paper.

Pick one team to go first and give them sixty seconds to guess as many of the names as possible. Take a player from the team and instruct them to take one piece of paper at random from the hat.

They then have to offer clues to their team about the name they have, without using the name itself, or spelling it out. Once someone from their team has guessed the name correctly, put that piece of paper aside and the player takes another name out of the hat and keeps going. At the end of the minute total up how many names the team has correctly identified. There are no passes, so if they don't know a name, they have to stick with it and try to find ways to let their teammates guess the name. For example, Baldrick: "a man with no hair is...? And a man's name that's short for Richard." If they don't guess the name they're on at the end of the minute, refold it and replace it in the hat.

At the end of the minute, the second team has its turn in a similar fashion, and then back to team one and so on. Keep on going in the same manner, making sure different players on the teams get a turn to be the clue giver until all the names are used. Total up the scores as you go along to determine the winner.

What's the purpose?

Possible learning/discussion point from this game:

- Do they feel known? By friends, family, local community, God?

11. The Introvert's ice-breaker

Theme connection: Judging others
Age suitability: 14+
Resources needed: Paper and pens, name labels
Venue requirements: None
Background preparation: None

The game

The announcement of an ice-breaker game is usually exciting for most young people – but not all. Those who don't relish interacting with strangers or people they don't know very well can often dread the experience. So this is a game for them, involving absolutely no talking and barely any interaction, which can still break the ice in an unfamiliar group.

Give everyone a sticker with their name on, which they should wear in a prominent position. Then give everyone a pen and a piece of paper, and invite them to walk around the venue, looking at each other (!). They should each choose a person whom they don't know, and write down their name and three things they think they can guess about that person just by looking at them. Possible guesses might include:

- They like comic book films.

- They're a vegetarian.

- They're into dance music.

- They do a certain school subject.

Once they've made three guesses for that person, they move on to the next person, and again make three guesses about them. The key is that they must choose people whom they don't know.

There is obviously a danger that this could lead to some unkind comments being written, so to avoid relational disaster make sure that you as the leader are the filter through which the comments are read. Once everyone has written comments for a few people, choose a volunteer and – scanning their paper for any inappropriate guesses – read their first person description out, along with the name of the person they were guessing about. Ask that person if any of the guesses were accurate – if they were, award a small prize to the person who guessed. Read through a few of the guess sheets – as quickly as possible – and keep going until interest wanes! The young people may then check their guesses with those they guessed about at your discretion.

What's the purpose?

Possible learning/discussion point from this game:

- We all make snap judgments about each other, and while they're occasionally correct, they're often wrong. We can overlook or mistreat certain people based on something we assumed about them – and this might not even be true.

12. I have never...

Theme connection: Truth, identity, community

Age suitability: 11+

Resources needed: None

Venue requirements: This game works best in an indoor space where there's room for everyone to sit on the floor

Background preparation: Make sure you've prepared your list of statements in advance – and that you have more than you think you'll need. This game shouldn't be left open to improvisation and making up statements on the spot, in case those statements become inappropriate

The game

Everyone in the room should find a space and stand in it. Explain that you're now going to read a list of pre-prepared statements, and everyone needs to decide whether each one is true of them or not. If a statement <u>is true</u> for them, then they should sit down; if the statement doesn't apply to them, they remain standing.

Start with a couple of test runs – for example a statement that no one can agree with (e.g. "I have never been to this youth group"), and then one which might divide the group in half (e.g. "I have never worn a dress"). Reset everyone to the standing position, and begin the game for real.

At first, read a few statements which will only cause a few people to sit down, for example:

- "I have never seen Toy Story."

- "I have never been to [insert name of fairly large nearby town]."

Then move on to a series of statements which is likely to bring your numbers down further, for example:

- "I have never left this country."

- "I have never eaten Thai food."

Finally, read some statements which are likely to be true of most people, for example:

- "I have never met a celebrity."

- "I have never been in the newspaper."

See if you can whittle the group down to just a single (and probably very interesting!) contestant. In all of this, make sure that none of your questions are in any way likely to cause offence or provoke teasing for those who respond to them.

What's the purpose?

Possible learning/discussion points from this game:

- Sometimes it can be a little embarrassing to tell the truth about ourselves, but honesty is key to good relationships.

- This game is also a good way into a general discussion about life choices, and decisions about how we spend our time. Do we try to do lots of interesting things, and attempt to have new experiences, or do we get stuck in the same patterns of behaviour?

13. Ping Pong Bounce

Theme connection: Challenge, perseverance

Age suitability: 7+

Resources needed: Ping pong balls, collection of boxes/cups/bowls/chamber pots/anything else a ping pong ball could fit into

Venue requirements: Hard surface (floor)

Background preparation: Loosely space out the receptacles, haphazardly or as creatively as your environment allows, and then mark out a line a couple of feet away (depending on the skill level/height of your participants) from which they have to bounce the ping pong balls into the cups. Allocate different points for each target, ranging from 100 to 10 points (dependent on ease of target)

The game

Allow five balls per participant, and get them to take it in turns to bounce the balls into the pots and score as highly as possible. Set the rule that the ball has to bounce on the ground before it goes into a pot and explain that if it misses everything it scores nothing. Keep score and award the top scorer a plastic cup in honour of their achievement.

Tip: This works best playing towards a wall as it allows for rebounds, and prevents any missed shots going miles! You could also use the wall to place receptacles at different heights for an extra challenge. You could play it as a team game if you have a bigger group, but it works best with a small number of players.

What's the purpose?

Possible learning/discussion points from this game:

- How easy do you find it to keep trying when something is difficult? Do you sometimes find yourself giving up? Why?

- Do you set targets for yourself? Why? Why not?

14. The Blanket game

Theme connection: Identity, community, teamwork

Age suitability: 9+

Resources needed: A large blanket or sheet

Venue requirements: None

Background preparation: None

The game

Divide the group into two teams randomly and separate them at opposite ends of the room. Between them erect a barrier (something like a large blanket or thick sheet held up by two leaders is ideal) and get one member of each team to come and stand on each side of the blanket without the opposite team seeing them. On the count of three drop the blanket and whichever of the two standing there can shout out the other person's name the quickest scores a point for their team. Send them back to their own teams, bring up another two people, and repeat. Keep playing till everyone has had a few turns.

Alternatively you can play it in such a way that the person who gets the other person's name first wins the other person over to join their team. This makes it more rewarding and exciting, but means that you have to play to a time limit as otherwise the game has the potential to be drawn out.

It's important that you ensure that your teams are far enough back that they cannot see which person from the opposing team is behind the blanket. If you don't have a big enough blanket available then it may be possible to play it from behind any kind of easily removable barrier, or even using a doorway.

What's the purpose?

Possible learning/discussion points from this game:

- If playing the variation where the "loser" swaps to the other team this could open up a discussion on what it means to be part of a team.

- How do they feel when people don't know their name?

15. Chinese mimes

Theme connection: Silence

Age suitability: 11+

Resources needed: Cards containing various simple charade phrases. The first should be a form of employment (Pizza Chef); the others are up to you

Venue requirements: None – in fact this is one game which can be played almost anywhere, and with as much background noise as you like

Background preparation: None

The game

Explain: we're going to practise sending messages to each other without speaking. Instead, we're going to communicate entirely through the power of mime... Therefore the whole activity should take place in near enough total silence.

Ask your group to line up, one behind the other, with a few feet of space between each person. It's important that everyone faces the same direction, and that no one (including you) speaks after you've explained that we're going to try passing a message from the back of the line to the front, by copying a mime. Do not mention that the subject of the mime will be a form of employment.

Go to the back of the line, and show the first person a card with the words "Pizza Chef" on it. Underneath you might also write something like "Act out doing this job". After they've practised, indicate for them to tap on the shoulder of the next person in the line, who turns around and watches the mime repeated.

They then tap on the shoulder of the next person and perform the mime to them. This carries on until you reach the person at the front of the line. This person then performs the mime to the whole group. Afterwards ask them: what job was this? They'll probably be surprised that this was even meant to be a mime of a job.

If you play further rounds, change the category but don't tell them! Second time around you could go for a sport such as badminton; third time around you could choose a mode of travel, like getting onto an aeroplane.

What's the purpose?

Possible learning/discussion points from this game:

- Although the game is hard, it's made easier when you're focused – and focus is easier when we're silent.

- Silence is difficult – they probably found it quite hard to maintain quiet once they'd had their turn in the game.

- Silence is an ancient Christian discipline which helps us to hear the voice of God. It's a simple theory: when we stop speaking, we give him a chance to speak!

Get Set, Go!

So, these chapter titles, Martin.

Yes, Jimmy.

What's the difference between, say, "Get Set, Go!" and "Quick-Fire Games"? They sound the same.

Ah, but that's exactly where you're wrong, my dog-collared friend. The distinction is simple, but important. As you'll discover later, the quick-fire section is all about games which can be played in a short period of time – say five minutes all in (if that's what you're looking for, head for chapter 12 now).

This chapter is all about games which can be played anywhere, with no preparation, and no resources. All you need is your wit and at least a few young people. In fact, this entire section was inspired by a recent incident at my house, when a 6 p.m. power cut made bedtime for my four children really fun/harrowing (delete as you believe to be true).

Short, sweet, and easy to play off the cuff, that's what you're saying? The kind of thing that you might keep in your mental toolkit of games to pull out of the bag at any time? Gotcha. (And by the way, a mental toolkit sounds like either the single best resource requirement that we will come up with for this book, or alternatively

*the kind of thing an imaginary AA repair man takes
around in his – imaginary – yellow van. Either way,
everyone should have one.)*

These aren't intended to discourage you from planning properly
– hopefully good resources never do that – but they can work as a
great emergency measure. If you've ever had to keep an excitable
group of young people occupied on a long minibus journey (or
in an airport lounge if you're operating at the higher budget end
of youth work), you'll know that this kind of activity can be the
difference between survival and despair. More regularly, they're
useful when your session on drawing meaning from the genealogies
runs unexpectedly short.

A word of warning though: because of their ease, these games can
quickly become a regular fixture in your youth programme. After all, it's
one less thing to have to think about in your planning. Unfortunately,
when we do that young people quickly tire of them and they lose their
power. This section is best used in moderation, then, and saved like a
Get Out of Jail Free card for when you need it most!

16. Celeb-abet

Theme connection: Celebrity, identity
Age suitability: 9+
Resources needed: None
Venue requirements: None
Background preparation: None

The game

An unbelievably "clever" combination of celebrity and alphabet, this
game pits two contestants against each other in a bid to find out who
can name the most celebrities.

Starting with Player One, and taking alternating turns, they each
have to name a celebrity whose name begins with successive letters
of the alphabet. So Player One has to name one beginning with A,
Player Two has to name one beginning with B, Player One then one
beginning with C, and so on. Give each player no more than five
seconds to come up with a name or they lose. If they manage to

get up to Z then simply restart at A again, but allowing no repeated celebrities.

To play this as a team game get all the players lined up in two teams, behind Player One and Player Two. Once either player loses a life they step aside and the person behind them steps up to carry on the game. Keep going until all the players from one team are eliminated.

What's the purpose?

Possible learning/discussion points from this game:

- Which celebrities do they look up to and why? Are they always good role models? Do they have any role models who are not famous?

- Discuss: what does it mean to be "known"?

17. Track the pulse

Theme connection: Communication, observation
Age suitability: 9+
Resources needed: None
Venue requirements: None
Background preparation: None

The game

Get your group to stand in a circle and hold hands with the people either side of them. Find a volunteer to be "it" – and send them out of the room while you pick someone in the circle to start the game.

Bring back your volunteer and then get your second person to secretly begin the pulse passing around the circle. The pulse is simply a squeeze of a hand, and moves around the circle in a consistent direction (i.e. it doesn't matter whether it's clockwise or anti-clockwise, as long as it keeps moving in the same direction).

The job of your first volunteer is to try to identify the pulse as it moves around the circle; give them three chances to find it before picking a new volunteer. They need to identify the person who is

33

passing on the pulse at that moment in order to count as a successful guess. To make the game fair hands must be displayed at all times, not hidden or obscured.

What's the purpose?

Possible learning/discussion points from this game:

- How observant do your group feel they are?

- We communicate in many ways, some of which we're not even concious of. Did you find yourself picking up on body language to try to find the pulse? Do you think you're normally aware of the body language?

18. Missing word whispers

Theme connection: Communication, listening, misunderstanding

Age suitability: 9+

Resources needed: None

Venue requirements: This game should take place in a quiet indoor venue if possible

Background preparation: None

The game

This is an upgraded version of the classic game Chinese Whispers. Get into groups of around five to begin with, and ask the groups to stand in lines. Ask the first person in each line to think of a short phrase of at least six or seven words.

Now ask the first young person to whisper that phrase to the second person. The second person whispers it into the ear of the third, but this time removes a word. The third person takes what they have heard, removes a word, and whispers it to the fourth, and so on.

By the time the message reaches the fifth person, it will have several words missing AND may have been mistranslated. They have to say what they think the original phrase might have been. If it goes well, try again with a longer phrase and bigger teams.

What's the purpose?

Possible learning/discussion point from this game:

- This game helps us to understand that when we communicate with each other, there's always plenty of room for misunderstanding – especially when we're not talking clearly, out loud, face to face.

19. Follow the cough

Theme connection: Discernment, distractions

Age suitability: 9+

Resources needed: Blindfold

Venue requirements: You need the venue to be as quiet as possible in order to make this game work. It's also important to play in a space where it is safe to be blindfolded (i.e. without lots of obstacles to trip over or possible places to bang your head)

Background preparation: None

The game

Ask a volunteer to step out of the room. Now choose up to six other volunteers who can cough/clear their throat on demand without it instigating a coughing fit (!). Nominate one of these as "The True Cough".

Spread these volunteers around your venue, then bring the first young person back into the room, blindfolded. Explain that they are going to have to try to pick out one person's cough among many, and move towards it. Put this person in the middle of the room (an echoing hall is ideal!) and make sure there are no obstacles or tripping hazards in their way.

Now ask "The True Cough" to cough three times. Explain to the blindfolded volunteer that this is the person they will need to move towards. Now spin them around several times, and tell your other volunteers that they are all allowed to cough. Your blindfolded volunteer must try to discern The True Cough and walk to them.

If you're concerned about the safety aspect of this game, use leaders as your coughing volunteers, or substitute whistling for coughing instead.

What's the purpose?

Possible learning/discussion points from this game:

- As Christians we all want to move towards God, rather than away from him, but there are lots of competing voices which are trying to distract us.

- Following God requires discernment: listening hard and attuning our ears to his voice.

20. How many footsteps?

Theme connection: Silence, discernment, listening to God

Age suitability: 11+

Resources needed: Blindfold, small chocolate prizes

Venue requirements: A fairly large, quiet venue, or one that can be temporarily made quiet (silent if possible). Ideally, this game will take place in a room with a hard, non-carpeted floor which amplifies footsteps, such as a church hall

Background preparation: None

The game

Choose one volunteer to be your "listener", and take them out of the room.

Now choose a number of young people (between one and five) to stand at one end of the room. Blindfold the volunteer, then bring them back in. Stand them in the middle of the room. You now need total silence from the group members who aren't playing the game.

Your non-blindfolded volunteers must walk, ideally without speaking, from one end of the room to the other. It would be good if they helped the listener by being fairly heavy-footed (!). The listener must try to work out how many people are walking past them, just by listening for different pairs of footsteps.

Award them a small chocolate prize if they guess correctly, then repeat the game with another volunteer. If your volunteers find the game too easy, repeat the exercise, but this time suggest your "walkers" are more light-footed as they walk across the room.

What's the purpose?

Possible learning/discussion points from this game:

- This is a fun way to introduce the concept of listening – and listening out for something quiet in near-silence.

- Hearing from God is difficult, but like all difficult things, the more we do of it, the better we get.

21. Bang bang, you're dead

Theme connection: Identity, violence

Age suitability: 9+

Resources needed: None

Venue requirements: None

Background preparation: None

The game

Get everyone to stand in a circle and choose one person (a leader is normally best the first few times you play this) to stand in the middle. That person then needs to call out the name of someone standing in the circle. Upon hearing their name called that second person has to duck quickly while the two people standing either side of them clasp their hands and fingers together in the shape of a gun, and point and shoot at each other, shouting "Bang" as loudly as your nerves can stand. If the person whose name was called doesn't duck quickly enough they "die" and sit down. If they have ducked in time whoever was the last of the two neighbours to shoot and shout (or whoever did it with insufficient enthusiasm/volume/panache, depending on how mean you are!) is judged to have been shot and sits down. (If it's too close to call then simply say they both got lucky and move on with everyone still in the game.)

As people are eliminated the fun increases, because the young people have to keep check of who they are standing next to (i.e. if their immediate neighbour is out of the game, their new neighbour is the next person standing). Continue the game until you are left with just two people. Depending on time/the competitive nature of your group you can either declare them both winners or have them "duel" it out. (This is a scenario that can be adapted to serve any game/ situation where you have two winners or finalists.) Get them to stand back to back and take a step forward each time you say the name of a vegetable, but when (eventually) you say a fruit they have to turn and shoot each other with their hands/fingers clasped in the shape of a gun.

This is a good game for getting people to learn each other's names without being too obvious about it too!

What's the purpose?

Possible learning/discussions points from this game:

- What do the young people think about the effect on them of constant exposure to violence in films/TV/video games?

- Sometimes we don't know the people around us. That makes this game difficult; what do you do in your everyday life to help you get to know new people?

22. Monkey-man-woman relay

Theme connection: Gender, sexism, power, justice

Age suitability: 9+

Resources needed: None

Venue requirements: None

Background preparation: None

The game

This is a variation on rock, paper, scissors, where instead of making the shape of rocks/paper/scissors with their hands they have to use their whole body to be either a monkey, a man, or a woman. The action for "monkey" is to pretend to be a huge gorilla (complete with chest beating and ape-like leaping); for "man" to do a James Bond-esque shooting of a gun and blowing on the barrel; and for "woman" to do a femme fatale style 1950s movie star shape with one hand on the hip, one hand behind the head, and a coy little bob of the knees. (The bigger the shapes and actions the better.) The gorilla beats the woman (the kidnapped damsel-in-distress of King Kong), the man beats the gorilla (also like in King Kong), and the woman defeats the man (just like in real life…).

Divide the group into two teams and send each team to opposite ends of the hall where they line up as in a relay race. Then call one player from each team to meet in the middle of the hall and play (if they are extra energetic give them three seconds or so, as appropriate, to run to the middle and if they don't make it in time then they lose before they've even started!). Give them a countdown from three and get them to simultaneously produce their shapes. The losing competitor is taken to the victor's team as spoils of war and joins their side, and the next pair are called up. If they produce the same shape then simply send them back to their own teams. The game can be played for an agreed period of time or until one team totally dominates.

What's the purpose?

Possible learning/discussion points from this game:

- What do they feel about the roles allocated to the different characters? Make sure you're clear that the game deliberately uses outdated stereotypes to introduce exactly this kind of discussion!

- How often do they encounter sexism in life?

23. Maths Monster

Theme connection: Challenge, planning ahead

Age suitability: 9+

Resources needed: None

Venue requirements: None

Background preparation: None

The game

Get everybody to pair off, and then face their partner with both hands behind their back. On the count of three they each need to produce one hand with a number of fingers extended (you might want to clarify what kind of gesture is acceptable!). The first of the pair to correctly identify the total number of fingers displayed on both hands – their own plus their opponent's – is the winner. You could then proceed with a knockout tournament to end up with an ultimate winner, or simply get the players to find new partners to mix them up a bit.

What's the purpose?

Possible learning/discussion points from this game:

- Maths is fun and/or useful – discuss!

- How much strategy do you employ in the way you conduct your everyday life? Do you think strategically about how you'll get your homework done, or even how you'll organize your social calendar, or do you leave it all to chance? Which approach do you think is better?

24. Loser

Theme connection: Bullying, challenge, faith

Age suitability: 9+

Resources needed: None

Venue requirements: None

Background preparation: None

The game

A game that works with any number from four up, as long as the young people can see each other easily. Get the group into a rough circle (so they can see each other) and pick one person to start the game. They do this by pointing at another person in the circle and saying their own name. That person then has to point at someone else, again saying their own name, and so on.

There are just three rules: 1) if you point back at the person who pointed at you, you become a loser and must sit for the rest of the game holding your hand in the universal loser sign on your forehead (right-handed, thumb and forefinger forming a right angle); 2) If you say a name other than your own while pointing at someone you become a loser (and hold your hand in the loser sign); 3) If you point at someone who is a loser, you become a loser (etc.). You might wish to enforce a speed rule to keep people from stalling for thinking time, but this game very rapidly becomes quite difficult. Keep on until there are only two people left, or everyone else gets bored!

Obviously any game named "Loser" can have negative undertones, so there is definitely something to be said for trying to ensure that any vulnerable young people don't end up labelled too enthusiastically as losers in this game. Participating yourself and taking a fall early on can be a good technique to relax any worried young people! (Although, let's face it, some youth leaders can be pretty competitive so this may be good for group dynamics anyway!)

What's the purpose?

Possible learning/discussion points from this game:

- Discussion starter: how does it feel to be labelled as a loser?

- What does the Christian faith have to say about what it really means to lose or win (think about Jesus' words about the first being last)?

25. What's the point?

Theme connection: Identity, bullying, justice

Age suitability: 9+

Resources needed: None

Venue requirements: Depending on the size of your space, you might want to adapt the game slightly to include less exaggerated movements (see below)

Background preparation: None

The game

Get everyone seated or standing in a circle (try to make it as much of a true circle as possible – for reasons of geometry and the need for everyone to be able to see everyone else, this is the optimal set-up!). On your instruction everyone in the circle needs to close their eyes, and then again on your command they need to silently use one arm to point at someone else in the circle. When you say so everyone opens their eyes, leaving their arm pointing in the same direction as they originally positioned it. Then tally up the number of "points" each person receives. Anyone receiving two or more points is out of the game. Repeat until you're left with just two people. Settle any disputed "pointings" by establishing in advance that any "pointings" that point at no one in particular are simply required to swing to the left until they are pointing at someone.

This could feel like a bit of a negative game, so careful management is needed to ensure that no one feels victimized. Also, if you are playing in a small room, or one with many ornaments (!) you could minimize any risk by adapting the arm point to a hand point.

As with any games that end up with two finalists that can't be separated by the original game, a duel technique is useful to decide the winner (position your finalists back to back, they take a step forward each time you as leader say something from a particular category, e.g. fruit, and then turn and shoot each other when you say a thing from a different category, e.g. a vegetable). Alternatively, toss a coin, or use any other way you like to choose a winner. (Drawing lots can always lead into an Old Testament Bible study on the use of the Urim and Thummim…)

What's the purpose?

Possible learning/discussion points from this game:

- Pointing is sometimes considered rude – how does it make you feel to be pointed at?

- Where do you get your sense of identity from? From what you think about yourself, from what others think about you, or something else (i.e. what God thinks)?

26. Inky Pinky Plonky Wonky

Theme connection: Planning ahead, challenge
Age suitability: 9+
Resources needed: None
Venue requirements: None
Background preparation: None

The game

Get your group standing in a circle with both hands outstretched, palms up, with their right hand resting on top of the left hand of the person on their right. (It sounds more complicated than it actually is – essentially you end up with everyone standing in a circle with their right hand resting on someone's hand, and someone else's hand resting on their left hand.)

The first person claps their right hand onto the hand resting on their left hand and says "inky", that person then claps their right hand onto the hand resting on their left saying "pinky", the next person does the same saying "plonky", the next person does the same while saying "wonky", and the fifth person then repeats the actions and says a number of their choosing, e.g. "six".

The subsequent people then count their way down from that number as they clap their hands in the same way ("five", clap; "four", clap; etc.) until someone says "one" as they clap their hand over. At this point the person whose hand is being clapped onto has to withdraw their hand before it can be clapped. If they fail and their hand is clapped while the person next to them is saying "one", then they are out. If they do succeed in withdrawing their hand before it's clapped they are still in, and start the whole process off again by clapping their hand and saying "inky", and so on. Keep going, knocking people out until you are left with a single winner.

Tip: put a sensible upper limit on the number they can pick, dependent on the size of your group.

What's the purpose?

Possible learning/discussion point from this game:

- Thinking ahead is a useful skill in this game – how does your group approach planning ahead in life?

27. Twenty Questions

Theme connection: Truth, identity

Age suitability: 9+

Resources needed: None

Venue requirements: None

Background preparation: None

The game

Choose someone in your group to start you off: they need to think of a person (famous, or at least known to the rest of the group) and everyone else takes it in turns to ask yes/no questions to try to work out who it is. If they can't do so within twenty questions the first person wins. If the group do guess correctly, the person who guessed gets to pick someone for the rest of the group to try to identify. Repeat as many times as you need!

What's the purpose?

Possible learning/discussion points from this game:

- What are the essentials that make up a person's identity? What matters more – appearance, occupations, actions, history, etc.?

- It would be much easier to win at this game if you were to lie; so always telling the truth can be costly.

28. Thirty seconds to know you

Theme connection: Identity, social media

Age suitability: 11+

Resources needed: None

Venue requirements: None

Background preparation: None

The game

Instruct your group to get into pairs and find themselves some space. Tell them to pick one of the pair as the target (T), and the other as the questioner (Q). The Targets then have thirty seconds to share as much information as they can about themselves on a topic that you as leader pick (e.g. holidays/family/favourite TV shows/school, etc.).

At the end of the thirty seconds split up the pairs, with all the Qs on one side of the room, and all the Ts on the other. Then ask the Qs a simple question relating to the topic chosen, for example, for family – how many brothers/sisters does your Target have? Check answers with the Targets, and any Qs that answered incorrectly sit down. Ask another simple question on the same topic, again eliminating any pairs that answer incorrectly, repeating until you have a winning pair. As this should be a fairly quick game it might be possible to return to it later in the session and swap roles within the pairs.

Tip: keep an eye out for any cheating/communication between Target and Questioner during questioning. Also try to be aware of, and treat sensitively, what may be sensitive topics to any of your group.

What's the purpose?

Possible learning/discussion points from this game:

- How well can you know someone? How quickly can you know someone?

- So much of our social interaction now happens in short bursts online – what do your group think are some of the positives and negatives of this?

29. Zip Zap Boing

Theme connection: Challenge, feeling overwhelmed
Age suitability: 9+
Resources needed: None
Venue requirements: None
Background preparation: None

The game

Get everybody into a circle and instruct them to place their hands together as if praying. Explain that a pulse is being passed around the circle and that when it comes to them they have to choose how it continues its journey by playing either a Zip, a Zap, or a Boing.

To zip you simply pass the pulse on in the same direction as it's already travelling by pointing your hands to the appropriate person beside you and saying clearly "Zip". If you want to reverse the pulse's direction, though, you simply "boing" it when it gets to you by clenching your fists, holding both arms upright, and saying "Boing". Finally if the pulse comes to you, you can choose to zap it to someone else in the circle by pointing your hands at them and saying "Zap".

Once your group pick up the basics of how this works and are adept at passing the pulse around at speed, introduce these competitive elements. They are very simple:

- You cannot zap a zap.

- You cannot boing a zap.

- You cannot boing a boing.

Also keep an eye out for pausing, getting the direction wrong after a Zap, or any other infringement as you feel appropriate. Eliminate people for any rule-breaking, including anyone who breaks the pace of the game, until you end up with three winners.

What's the purpose?

Possible learning/discussion point from this game:

- Sometimes the pace of life can seem unsustainable – how do you cope with this?

30. The Animal Game

Theme connection: Creation
Age suitability: 9+
Resources needed: None
Venue requirements: None
Background preparation: None

The game

Get your group seated in a horseshoe formation. Explain that each seat represents an animal in the food chain and that the positions at the ends of the horseshoe are the top and bottom of the food chain, the lion and the amoeba (you may want to skate over the biological aspects of this game).

The aim of the game is to progress as high up the food chain as possible and to remain there. Explain that each animal has an action and a noise to represent it, and demonstrate with the lion and the amoeba. Get the person on the chair representing the lion to roar while holding their hands in the shape of claws, and the person on the amoeba chair to make a wobbly shape with their hands while calling out "gloop gloop".

Now get everybody else to decide what animal their chair should represent and what their noise/action should be. Be ready with ideas should they get stuck, or to inspire. For example, mosquito – "bzzz" and slap your arm as if squashing one; giraffe – arm extended above head with hand making a mouth, and make a chewing noise; eagle – flap arms and make a majestic eagle call (!); dolphin – move your hand in a wave motion and make a dolphin-like clicking sound; elephant – extend your arm from your nose and make a trumpeting sound, and so on.

Make sure each action and noise is clear and distinct and get each person to demonstrate to the rest of the group to give them a chance to learn the others' animals. Emphasize that each animal is connected to a specific chair and hence position in the food chain.

The way the game works is by the Lion starting off with their action and noise, followed by the action/noise of whomever they are passing it to (which could be any other animal in the game). That person then does their animal noise/action plus the noise/action of whom they pass it to and so on. The only rules are that you cannot pass back to the person who passed it to you, you have to do the actions/noises as accurately as possible, and you mustn't break the rhythm, not even for fits of laughter (which is a high risk factor in this game!).

If someone fails to do this, they get relegated to the amoeba position, and everyone who was below them in the food chain moves up one seat, adopting the action/noise of their new seat. The person who fills the highest empty seat then continues the game in the same way as before.

It's probably worth playing a trial round just so people get the idea before sending people to the bottom of the chain, and once they've got it this is a game that can run and run for as long as you like. It works best with groups anywhere between six and twenty, but can be played with any number although difficulty arises in trying to think of distinct animal actions and noises with larger numbers! If you have a large group you could consider dividing into two separate games, and then if you wanted you could take the top half of each chain and play them off against each other to find an ultimate animal champion.

What's the purpose?

Possible learning/discussion points from this game:

- Why do they think God's creation is so varied and extravagant?

- How well do we do at the task of "looking after" creation?

31. Weeping angels

Theme connection: Fear, challenge, faith

Age suitability: 11+

Resources needed: None

Venue requirements: A room with an easily accessible light switch

Background preparation: None

The game

If your young people have seen any of the recent few series of *Doctor Who*, then chances are they will have come across "The Weeping Angels". These are baddies of the highest level of genius and scariness – statues that can move when no one is looking, and send their unsuspecting victim back in time (in order to feed off their temporal energy, or something. Try not to think about that bit too much, or it all falls apart in a mush of timey-wimey related nonsense!). Why not display a modicum of cultural relevance by taking an old favourite playground game (What's the Time Mr Wolf?) and "ironically" re-contextualizing it for an older, and more sci-fi savvy crowd?

Simply position one player by the light switch, and place all the other players at the far end of the room. Explain that they are the "weeping angels" and their task is to sneak up and catch the player by the light switch. The rules are: they can only move when the light is off, and if the player sees them move when the light is on they are eliminated. If any of the angels get up to the player and tag them, then they get to have a go at being the player by the light switch, and the game resets with all the angels reinstated and returned to the far end of the room as before.

What's the purpose?

Possible learning/discussion points from this game:

- Fear of the unknown – discuss.

- What does it mean that "The light shines in the darkness, and the darkness has not overcome it" (John 1:5)?

32. Shoelace Chain Race

Theme connection: Connections (quite "meta", this one)

Age suitability: 9+

Resources needed: People to be wearing footwear with some kind of lace

Venue requirements: None

Background preparation: Do give warning in advance to the young people that you are going to play this game, and be sensitive to any who have issues with feet/socks, etc.

The game

Divide your group into two teams and then get them to take off all their shoes and heap them together (as a team) at one end of your hall. Then get teams to swap piles and instruct them to randomly pair shoes together and tie the laces together. (You might want to get leaders to oversee this to ensure the knots aren't tied too tightly to subsequently untie!) Make clear they don't need to worry about whether the shoes match, or even include a left and a right, simply that each shoe is paired with one other. Then send the teams to the other end of the hall, and get them lined up as for a relay race.

Explain that once you start the race the first person has to run to their team's pile of shoes, find one of their own shoes, and put it on. They then return to their teammates where the person whose shoe is attached to the first person's shoe has to put their shoe on and join the first person. Together, they then return to the pile of shoes where the new person finds their other shoe and puts that on, before returning to the rest of the team where the person whose shoe is paired with that shoe slips it on, joins the chain, returns to the pile, finds their other shoe, and so on...

Eventually you should end up with a chain of people attached by the laces of their shoes, some of whom are probably facing different directions as right shoes are paired with left shoes and so forth, shuffling up and down the hall. You might find that you end up completing a chain without all the teammates being attached, in which case the chain needs to return to their teammates, and link arms with one at random who returns with them to the pile of shoes, finds one of theirs, puts it on, and then linked to the completed chain shuffles back to the team to find their shoe's partner's foot...

All very chaotic and good fun! The winning team is of course the first team to have all teammates fully shod and connected, and back at the start line.

What's the purpose?

Possible learning/discussion point from this game:

- "Everything eventually connects" – do your group think this is true in life? Do they see connections between different areas of life? Different people? Different situations?

33. Follow my Leader

Theme connection: Leadership, following
Age suitability: 9+
Resources needed: None
Venue requirements: None
Background preparation: None

The game

Get everyone sitting in a circle, and pick one person to leave the room. Explain that while they are outside you are going to choose one of the remaining people to be the leader of the group, and the absent person's task on returning to the room is to work out who that leader is. The rule is that everyone must copy exactly what the leader does, so you get everyone scratching their nose, or tapping their feet, or crossing their legs, etc. The guesser then has three opportunities to name the leader. Repeat.

What's the purpose?

Possible learning/discussion points from this game:

- Is it easier to lead or follow in this game? What about in life?
- When "leading" did people feel pressure?

34. Hot air balloon

Theme connection: Consumerism, community
Age suitability: 9+
Resources needed: None
Venue requirements: None
Background preparation: None

The game

Get your group sitting in a circle and explain that you are going to go on a (metaphorical) hot air balloon ride, and that as a group you need to decide what you are going to take with you. Get them to use the formula "On my hot air balloon trip I will take…, but not…", and suggest one thing they would take, and one thing they wouldn't. You as group leader then get to tell them whether what they decide to take or not is acceptable.

Proceed around the circle giving everyone a chance to suggest what they might like to take, and what to leave, confirming when they pack something acceptable or leave the right object, or telling them "no" when they get it wrong. As this progresses they will hopefully work out that you are using a specific rule to decide, and their challenge is to try and work out what this rule might be. Make sure that they know they shouldn't blurt out the rule if they think they've worked it out, but to test it instead to give everyone a chance to work it out. If your group are struggling to work it out, when it gets to your turn in the circle make your examples really extreme and unconnected so they can see which elements of what you say are important.

The simple rule is that you take things where the word has double letters (e.g. rabbit, kitten, balloon, etc.) and leave things without this. So you could start with "On my hot air balloon trip I will take a kitten, but not a dog."

What's the purpose?

Possible learning/discussion points from this game:

- What would you actually take if you could only take one possession?

- Would you describe yourself as materialistic? Why?

- How does it feel to be the person who doesn't understand when everyone else does? How should that impact our treatment of others?

35. Masterpiece

Theme connection: Gratitude, manners

Age suitability: 9+

Resources needed: Although this game requires nothing but the imagination, it can be helpful if you have something that can play the role of a paintbrush (a pen/pencil will do well, or just a stick if you're really struggling for things)

Venue requirements: None

Background preparation: None

The game

Get your group sitting in a horseshoe shape and stand in the middle of it, as if there is a giant canvas for you to paint on stretched across the gap. Hold a "paintbrush" in your hand and flourish it as if you are some sort of artistic genius. Proclaim that you are in the process of creating a masterpiece, and make a few movements as if you are painting a picture. Tell your group that you'd like them to help you out, and to see if they've got any artistic skills.

Get one of them to come up and take the "paintbrush" and pretend to add something to your picture – after which you tell them whether they are creating a masterpiece or not. Go around the group and give everyone a chance to have a go, and continue until they manage to work out what it is that they do that makes their "painting" a masterpiece or not. The rule is that if they say "thank you" when they receive the "paintbrush", whatever they paint is a masterpiece, and if not, it isn't.

What's the purpose?

Possible learning/discussion point from this game:

- Do manners matter? Does gratitude?

36. Have you seen Miss Marple?

Theme connection: Challenge, asking questions, judgment
Age suitability: 9+
Resources needed: None
Venue requirements: None
Background preparation: None

The game

Get your group sitting in a circle, and explain that in this game there are two key rules. Firstly, that at no time can you ever show your teeth, and secondly, that you cannot point with anything other than an elbow. With these two rules in mind explain that you are going to progress around the circle asking each other a set of questions... Person A asks their neighbour: "Have you seen Miss Marple?" Person B responds, "Miss Marple?" Person A: "Yes, have you seen Miss Marple?" Person B says, "I don't know, I'll ask my neighbour." At this point they become Person A and turn to their neighbour and repeat the whole process. Repeat *ad infinitum*. If at any stage someone accidentally shows their teeth, anyone who sees it can point at them (with their elbows) and call "teeth, teeth". Equally if someone points with a finger, or anything other than an elbow, then people can point at them (with elbows) calling out "pointing, pointing".

When people are caught breaking these rules you can start to eliminate them to find an ultimate winner. Alternatively, you can just play this game as a simple but silly bit of fun without elimination.

What's the purpose?

Possible learning/discussion points from this game:

- Complete this sentence: Asking questions in life is...

- Jesus talks about being careful not to point out the flaw in someone else without recognizing our own failings... How easy or difficult do the group think it is?

3

Challenges

My eight-year-old daughter can turn anything into a competition. Throwing, spelling, tidying up; if you turn it into a challenge, she's immediately interested. Naomi is naturally one of those people who draws motivation from competing against others; it's a brilliant trait which she absolutely didn't get from me. I'm the sort of sportsman who is much more likely to give up than give chase, and I'm thankful that my children are much more like their mother in this regard.

Although there are plenty of young people who share my sense of competitive defeatism, there are many more who get motivated and energized by a challenge. This set of games is for them.

> *A small warning – there is always the risk of becoming the hyper-competitive youth worker. These are competitions for the young people to engage with – not for you to demonstrate your prowess at peeling a banana with your toes (makes a mental note of an idea for a future game…).*
>
> *Finding the balance between a fun challenge and destructive competitiveness is a fine line too – be careful what you unleash with these games (wow, that sounds like a portent of doom… and time to make another mental note for a future game title) and don't allow that competition to become the defining feature of your session.*

Still, if you manage to keep the testosterone under control, there's often no more sure-fire way to get teenagers' attention than engaging their competitiveness. As long as you vary the nature of the challenges (so you're not always holding competitions which only test speed or strength for example), then a bit of healthy challenge can be a fun regular addition to your youth group sessions.

Also, it's worth saying that not all young people enjoy taking part in these kinds of games, but almost all enjoy watching them. The chance to cheer on their friends/laugh as their enemies lose[4] will be incredibly energizing for many young people who would never dream of volunteering to take part. This set of games is great for getting a whole group buzzing with excitement.

37. Turn the Raft

Theme connection: Challenge, community

Age suitability: 9+

Resources needed: Tarpaulin (or groundsheet/large rug, etc.)

Venue requirements: Enough space to lay your tarpaulin flat on the ground

Background preparation: None

The game

Lay your sheet out flat on the ground and get your group to stand on it. Explain that they are actually standing on a raft in the middle of the Pacific Ocean, surrounded by shark-infested waters, and that for some reason (that has temporarily escaped your mind) they need to turn the raft over so that they are all standing on the other side of it.

Explain that no one is allowed to touch the water, and if anyone is "lost" overboard they need to restart the process. Allow them to work out suitable techniques for supporting each other and keeping them all onboard. If they find it too easy, try reducing the size of the "raft" available.

---

4   Obviously we don't want to encourage this sort of thing.

What's the purpose?

Possible learning/discussion points from this game:

- A discussion about supporting each other could arise naturally out of this. (Or alternatively a reflection on the nature of pointless tasks.)

- This could also lead into a session on survival, skills, and working together.

38. Hang-Time

Theme connection: Challenge, longevity

Age suitability: 9+

Resources needed: A plentiful supply of paper, information on how to make a paper aeroplane, a stopwatch

Venue requirements: Enough space to throw paper aeroplanes

Background preparation: None

The game

Get everybody to make themselves a paper aeroplane, and divide the group into groups of four. Explain that these are their qualifying groups. One group at a time, they will all have to throw their paper planes (ensuring that they throw at the same time), and the planes which stay in the air the longest will qualify for the timing rounds. (Make sure you have plenty of leaders and helpers to keep track of which planes are the last to "land".) Depending on how many players you have overall you might want to adjust how many planes qualify out of each group – the intention should be to arrive at a final group of about four who have qualified – so adjust your qualification bar accordingly!

Once you have your final four, time their flights individually to find the best two, and then set them to fly head-to-head in a final Hang-Time battle. Get them to throw the aeroplanes at exactly the same time, and the one whose plane remains in the air the longest wins.

What's the purpose?

Possible learning/discussion points from this game:

- Do the group see any value in longevity?

- Does life reward those who stick around, or is it actually the other way round?

- What do you think God wants?

39. Share or steal

Theme connection: Honesty, greed, justice, Christian values

Age suitability: 7+

Resources needed: Four blank cards (approx. A5 size), marker pen, large chocolate bar (the more delicious, the better!)

Venue requirements: None

Background preparation: In big, clear type, write the word "share" in the middle of two of your cards, and "steal" in the middle of the other two. Pick your volunteers for this game carefully, so that you are unsure of what the result would be (don't pick two angelic types!)

The game

Choose two volunteers, and give each of them a "share" and a "steal" card. Tell them that there's a delicious chocolate bar available to them – but they have to agree to share it. They can then have a conversation (in front of everyone) to convince one another that they are indeed going to share it, rather than try to have it all for themselves. Give each person thirty seconds, in front of the group, to try to convince their friend/rival that they are going to agree to share.

However, each of them also possesses a "steal" card. At the end of their discussion, if they both hold up "share" cards, the chocolate is shared. However, if one of them holds up "share" and the other "steal", the whole chocolate bar goes to the "stealer"! There's a twist though – if they both try to steal, then neither of them gets the chocolate…

Have fun with the theatre of this before each person reveals their chosen card. Who do the crowd think is more likely to try to steal the whole bar? What do they think the outcome might be? If they're enjoying the debate, make sure you drag out the reveal as long as possible!

What's the purpose?

Possible learning/discussion points from this game:

- It's better to share. Sometimes the world is dishonest – but if we all follow that example, we'll have even bigger problems.

- This is a simple and fun way to introduce the topic of justice and sharing resources.

- In Mark 9:35 Jesus tells the disciples that "Anyone who wants to be first must be the very last." If we're committed to submitting to one another out of reverence for Christ (Ephesians 5:21), we should throw away our "steal" cards altogether, even if that means missing out on the whole chocolate bar!

40. Nice or nasty?

Theme connection: Greed, fear, choices

Age suitability: 11+

Resources needed: Two plates, a minimum of two spoons, two blindfolds, an array of spoonable foodstuffs – some nice, some not so nice. Examples might include ketchup, cold baked beans, other sauces, chocolate spread, honey, jam

Venue requirements: None

Background preparation: It is very important that you are aware of any food allergies before selecting volunteers for this game. If in doubt, use adult leaders/helpers. Before the session, prepare two identical plates of foodstuffs – some of them delicious, some of them less so, and some in the middle. Depending on your age group you may decide to be kinder, and whoever you're working with, stay away from the chilli sauce...

The game

Choose two volunteers with strong stomachs and adventurous taste buds. Blindfold them, and then sit them in front of a plate. Make sure everyone watching can see what's on there, but don't tell the blindfolded young people.

Now take two spoonfuls of one item, and ask both volunteers if they would like to taste it. If they both say yes, give it to them simultaneously; if they both say no, tell them what they missed out on. If one says yes, and the other no, give it to the one who asked for it, and let his or her reaction tell the other volunteer if they avoided a treat or something unpleasant.

Repeat for the rest of the plate. Alternatively, if lots of young people want to have a go, change the volunteers after every two items.

What's the purpose?

Possible learning/discussion point from this game:

- Everything is permissible, but not everything is beneficial (1 Corinthians 10:23); God has given us free will to do whatever we like in this life, but it's not always good for us or pleasant as a result.

41. Wind Tunnel Challenge

Theme connection: Overcoming challenges, activism

Age suitability: 9+

Resources needed: Enough paper for each player to make a paper aeroplane, pens, as many electrical fans of various sizes as you can source

Venue requirements: As long a length of free space as you can find indoors

Background preparation: Along the longest space you have available place as many electric fans of various sizes as you can at random intervals, to create your wind-tunnel. Angle them so they create inconsistent air-flows.

The game

Divide your group into teams of 4 or 5 and get each team member to construct a paper aeroplane, which they should then mark with a team emblem or colour. Explain that the challenge to your teams will be to see which of them can get their planes to fly the furthest distance along the "wind-tunnel".

One at a time allow the teams to try to throw their planes along the tunnel, awarding points to the teams whose planes get furthest along it.

Once your teams have managed to work out the best techniques for this (allow them to repeat a number of times to work this out as a team), rearrange your fans so that they are all on one side, and blowing the same way directly across the "wind-tunnel". Now see if any of your teams can get their planes to turn a right-angle using these as aids.

Finally, get your teams to all work together to try and divert the flight of one plane by simply using the power of their (collective) breath. Get them all grouped together in one spot, and gently throw a plane past them, and get them to try to blow in unison to affect the flight of the plane as much as possible. (They probably won't be able to, but it might be fun to try!)

What's the purpose?

Possible learning/discussion points from this game:

- Overcoming obstacles is an important part of life. How do you deal with these challenges?

- The game is all about working together to change the course of something. Do you believe you can change the world – and are you more likely to do that alone, or with others?

42. Marshmallow construction

Theme connection: Creativity

Age suitability: 9+

Resources needed: Many toothpicks/cocktail sticks, a packet of marshmallows (of the big and fluffy variety) per two or three players

Venue requirements: None

Background preparation: None

The game

Get your group into small groups (of two or three, exact numbers don't matter, but for the sake of maximum involvement small is best).

Give each group a full packet of marshmallows and as many toothpicks as they want, and get them to make the most creative 3D sculpture they can in five minutes. Allow them to consume their creations at the end.

What's the purpose?

Possible learning/discussion points from this game:

- Do you see yourself as a creative individual?

- What do you want to "construct" with your life?

43. Vegetable bobbing

Theme connection: Perseverance, the Bible

Age suitability: 11+

Resources needed: Two fairly deep buckets full of water; small chocolate prize; pairs of some or all of the following vegetables: Brussels sprout, parsnip, courgette, a single pea, onion (!); optional gentle hand ties, e.g. scarves; plastic mats or towels to catch water

Venue requirements: You must be in a venue where it doesn't matter if things get wet... Outside may work best

Background preparation: Some vegetables float – others don't – and you need floaters to make this game work! Fill your two buckets with water in advance of the session, and check that all of the vegetables you've chosen actually work. Sometimes one onion will float and another won't, so make sure you check every single item

The game

Apple bobbing is good… but it doesn't encourage participants to eat their greens like this game. Ask two volunteers who don't mind getting wet to come to the front of your venue, and sit each behind a bucket (those with long hair may need a friend to hold it out of the water).

Ask them to put their hands behind their backs (you could tie them gently with scarves or similar), then explain that they have to retrieve various vegetables from the buckets, faster than their opponents. Put the first vegetables into the buckets – start with something fairly easy like a parsnip – then shout "go".

Only when one of the young people passes you a vegetable with their mouth (they can't use hands at all) can you put the next vegetable into their bucket. It's then a race to see who can get through the entire list of vegetables first. Award a small prize to the victor.

What's the purpose?

Possible learning/discussion points from this game:

- Some things are harder than they look. The question then is: do we possess the strength of character to be able to persevere and see those things through?

- Perseverance is a biblical virtue which produces character (see James 1 for details). It's something which none of us cherishes – but actually the Bible tells us to do exactly that if we want to become fully formed people!

44. Total trust

Theme connection: Trust, submission

Age suitability: 11+

Resources needed: Crash mat, small chocolate prizes

Venue requirements: You MUST establish a really safe place to play this game – ideally standing on a thick crash mat. You're going to be responsible for catching young people as they fall, so make sure you insure against any mistakes!

Background preparation: Perform a risk assessment before playing this game

The game

Ask the young people: do they trust you? Pick a volunteer who says they do, and ask them to stand in front of you on the crash mat, with their back to you. Now, they have to rock back onto their heels, and fall backwards into your arms, crucially without trying to break their own fall (by bending their legs, putting their arms out to catch themselves, etc.). This is actually quite difficult – our natural instinct is to stop ourselves.

Once you've found someone who's prepared to do this, get them to fall, and get the rest of the group to judge whether they really did trust you completely. If the group think they did, give them a small chocolate prize. If not, ask for another volunteer, until you find someone who completely submits to you, and trusts you will catch them.

What's the purpose?

Possible learning/discussion points from this game:

- Who do you trust? Who do you trust enough to let them catch you?

- What does it mean to trust God? This activity was about submission – learning to let go of control and totally trusting God to meet our needs.

45. UFO Chocolate

Theme connection: Challenge, breath of life

Age suitability: 9+

Resources needed: Maltesers

Venue requirements: Enough space for your group to lie down

Background preparation: Buy enough Maltesers for your group, and a few spare ones in case you fancy a snack...

The game

Get the young people to lie down on their backs and give them each a Malteser. The aim of this activity is to see if, by blowing steadily and with the right amount of power, they can get the Malteser to "hover" in the air above their lips. (The technique is to place the Malteser on pursed lips and blow gently and consistently.) Keep a close eye, you don't want anyone to choke.

You could simply run this activity en masse for the fun of it, run it as a competition by timing each of the young people to see how long they can keep the Malteser in the air to find an overall winner, or run it as a head-to-head challenge upfront.

It could also be a team challenge, where you split the group into two teams, and create pairs with a player from each team. Get each pair to compete head to head, and award a point to the winning team within each pair to find the overall winners.

What's the purpose?

Possible learning/discussion points from this game:

- Do your young people feel that they are able to "control" their lives?

- The Bible uses imagery of the "breath of God" in creation (e.g. breathing into Adam, the wind of God moving over the waters, and so on). How does this imagery make your group feel? What does it make them think of? Is this useful imagery when we're thinking of God?

46. Plate Minds Think Alike!

Theme connection: Trust, consumption, justice, choices

Age suitability: 9+

Resources needed: Four plates, a selection of fruit, some milk and biscuits, a McDonald's Happy Meal, ice cream, fruit smoothie (optional), milkshake (optional), an electric food blender

Venue requirements: None

Background preparation: Before the group arrives place four plates around your room, one in each corner. On one of the plates place a selection of fruits, on another place a small bottle of milk and some chocolate biscuits, on one of them place a McDonald's Happy Meal, and leave the fourth plate empty. Set up your blender. Check food allergies

The game

Explain to your group that on your command, they need to go and stand by the plate they would like to consume. Make sure they know once they have made their final choice they are committed to it.

Once everyone has chosen their corner, produce a blender and proceed around the room. At plate one blend the fruits from the first plate together to make a smoothie, and pour into glasses as appropriate for the number of people who selected that corner. (Or you could buy a fruit smoothie from the supermarket beforehand to save time/effort/cleaning…)

At the plate with the milk and biscuits, blend them together (with some ice cream) to create an Oreo milkshake (or again buy a pre-made one).

Explain to the people by the empty plate that they get nothing, but on arriving finally at the plate with the Happy Meal place the burger, fries, and drink into the blender and mix it all up. Provide straws and see how much the unlucky punters can consume – but don't force them. (Make sure you get the milkshake as a drink, as it works much better in a blender than the fizzy drinks.) Enjoy the puzzled expressions and disgusted faces. (It doesn't actually taste that bad…)

What's the purpose?

Possible learning/discussion points from this game:

- Do any of the young people regret their choice?

- How did they feel about the blend of everything in the Happy Meal?

- Did this seem a fair activity?

47. Play your cards correctly

Theme connection: The future

Age suitability: 9+

Resources needed: Pack of playing cards

Venue requirements: None

Background preparation: None

The game

Take a normal pack of playing cards and lay out about a dozen of them face down in a row. Select two individuals to play against each other (or to represent two teams). Toss a coin to see who gets control of the board at the start, and flip over a card from the top of the pack. Ask the first player whether the first face down card will be higher or lower than that card, and once they make their choice reveal the card. If they are correct they keep control of the game and progress along to the next card, etc. If they get it wrong, however, control passes to their opponent who gets to decide whether they think the next card will be higher or lower, and so forth. The winner is the one who is in play at the end of the game.

Remember aces are high, and that you get nothing for a pair, not in this game...

What's the purpose?

Possible learning/discussion points from this game:

- Is there any point in trying to predict the future?

- Do your group ever try to do so – consciously or unconsciously?

- Do you think God knows the future? And if so, is the future set?

48. Human Bop-it

Theme connection: Teamwork, influence on the world
Age suitability: 9+
Resources needed: None
Venue requirements: None
Background preparation: None

The game

The human version of the popular game! Get your group into pairs where one partner acts as the machine, and the other plays the operator. Get the "machine" to stand comfortably, with the right hand up as if high-fiving someone, and the left hand clenched in a fist and extended horizontally from the body. The operator has to follow your instructions and do certain actions with the machine:

"Grab it" – grab both hands of the machine;
"Spin it" – spin the machine round on the spot;
"Bop it" – high-five the right hand;
"Pull it" – pull the machine's left arm down as if it were a lever on a one-armed bandit fruit machine.

Shout out the instructions at random in a steady rhythm, gradually increasing speed as you go along. Eliminate any pairs that miss or do actions incorrectly until you have a winning pair.

What's the purpose?

Possible learning/discussion points from this game:

- This could open up general discussion on the young people's sense of agency in the world.

- Can they think of examples of times when they have had a positive effect on the world around them? How did they feel?

49. Interpretive Dance

Theme connection: Creativity, communication

Age suitability: 11+

Resources needed: An MP3 player with headphones, loaded with songs full of expressive language

Venue requirements: Space to dance (!)

Background preparation: Preselect a song with plenty of expressive language and cue it up on the MP3 player. Identify a member of your group who will be able to "dance expressively", and not mind potentially making a fool of themselves

The game

Give the MP3 player to one of the more "creative" members of the group, along with instructions that, using only their mime/interpretive dance moves, they must communicate the song to the rest of the group. Give them some time to listen to the track/read the lyrics while you brief the rest of the group on their role (you could let your performer know the song in advance of the session to maximize the preparation time).

Tell the rest of the group that they are about to see a famous song being performed without sound, and that their task is to try to work out what the song is through the interpretative dance moves.

Once your performer is ready, get them to pop on the headphones and perform to the group (making sure that your group can't hear any of the song from the headphones) and allow your group to try to identify the track.

Make sure you use music that your group will be familiar with – if you don't think it's too sacrilegious you could use pretty much any modern worship song.

What's the purpose?

Possible learning/discussion point from this game:

- This could lead into a discussion on communication, creativity, or even the content of worship songs.

50. Pillow Ninja

Theme connection: Challenge, war

Age suitability: 11+

Resources needed: A pile of pillows

Venue requirements: Enough space to throw pillows, and to swat them

Background preparation: Gather your pillows and clear your playing space of any breakables

The game

Choose a player to stand at the front, and then from about five feet away, get the rest of the group to throw pillows towards them until you manage to get one to hit them on the body. The player's job obviously is to stop this from happening, and so using only their arms they can swipe and swoosh to prevent the pillows from hitting them. A plentiful supply of pillows/cushions is useful for this game, and different sizes present additional challenges.

Only allow one person to actually throw a pillow at a time initially – if your player is too good then increase the number of pillows that can be thrown simultaneously (for obvious reasons do not allow head shots and discount any that accidentally hit the head region). Once a player is hit on their body they are out and replaced by another player.

(The more discerning amongst you will realize that this game is essentially throwing pillows at someone to try to hit them. This may be true, but doesn't stop it from being enormous fun. Take that, cutting-edge video game technology!)

What's the purpose?

Possible learning/discussion point from this game:

- Discussions on the battle between good and evil, and spiritual warfare could arise from this game.

51. Box racing

Theme connection: Challenge, limitations
Age suitability: 9+
Resources needed: Enough boxes for one per player
Venue requirements: Enough room in which to hold a race
Background preparation: Have a trial "race" with your leaders

The game

Give an open box to each of your young people, and get them to stand in a line, inside their box. On your instruction get them to race to the other end of the room by means of shuffling/jumping/wobbling/

whatever. It is worth trying this out yourself first in your meeting room because, a) it's fun, and b) you will want to check how easy or hard it is to move on your room's floor, to ensure it's safe.

What's the purpose?

Possible learning/discussion points from this game:

- What limitations do your young people encounter in their daily lives?

- What parallels can they find in their everyday life with trying to race while stuck in a box?

52. Building Blocks

Theme connection: Creativity, building

Age suitability: 9+

Resources needed: As many empty boxes as you can gather

Venue requirements: A room tall enough to construct an arch

Background preparation: Gather the boxes, and ensure they are all taped shut

The game

The thing about boxes is that, basically, if they're taped shut at both ends, they are just large building blocks, and who doesn't love playing with building blocks? A challenge, therefore, for those young people who are more creative than competitive is to give your group a large pile of those boxes and get them to build a free-standing arch.

Explain that the challenge is to balance the boxes to create an arch large enough for one of the leaders to pass underneath it as comfortably as possible (they may interpret this in any number of ways!). If you have a large group (and enough spaces and boxes!) you can divide your group up and get them to build arches simultaneously as a race, or if you don't have enough space/boxes, get one group building while you take the rest off to do something else.

What's the purpose?

Possible learning/discussion points from this game:

- Do your young people feel that they are building things in their lives?

- Do they consider themselves to be creative?

53. Blindfold banana whacker (or "Are you there, Moriarty?")

Theme connection: Darkness, war, justice

Age suitability: 9+

Resources needed: Two inflatable bananas, two blindfolds, a sock

Venue requirements: Enough space for two people to lie down, head to head

Background preparation: None

The game

Based on an old Victorian parlour game (not the inflatable banana bit, unless the Victorians were a lot more fun than their image portrays), this game involves the two aforementioned players being blindfolded, and lying, tummy down, on the ground head-to-head a couple of feet apart.

Get the players to hold a sock between them (to keep them from getting too far apart) and in their other hands each holds an inflatable banana.

The game starts when Player A asks, "Are you there, Moriarty?" When they're ready Player B responds "Yes", at which point Player A gets one attempt to hit Player B with their banana. Player B is at this stage free to roll to one side or the other, or not at all, to try to dodge the blow (any move like this is fine as long as they stay connected via the sock, and remain lying on the ground).

Swap roles and repeat a couple of times, and then get two new volunteers to face off.

If you can't get hold of an inflatable banana, then a long sock stuffed with rolled-up newspaper doubles up well.

What's the purpose?

Possible learning/discussion points from this game:

- Do they ever feel like they are battling in the dark?

- (Banana Tangent Alert) Given the choice, would they be more likely to buy Fair Trade bananas, or slightly cheaper non Fair Trade ones?

54. Cracker Whistle

Theme connection: Challenge, communication

Age suitability: 9+

Resources needed: Packet of cream crackers; or hot chocolate powder for the alternative version

Venue requirements: None

Background preparation: Get some cups of water ready for your players to drink after they've competed

The game

Give each player a cracker, and explain that this is a race where on your mark they need to eat the whole cracker and then produce a clean and audible whistle. Start them off, and enjoy a relatively peaceful few minutes as they try, and fail, to whistle! Although the requirements for this game are minimal, you might want a dustpan and brush to sweep up the shards of cracker that will inevitably fill your space!

Alternatively, repeat the challenge with a dessertspoonful of hot chocolate powder. After putting it into their mouths they will be judged by the rest of the group on how clearly they can say a sentence such as, "My youth leader is amazing, and when I grow up I want to be just like them." (Or any other equally plausible and affirming statement that you can come up with.) They'll find this incredibly difficult.

What's the purpose?

Possible learning/discussion points from this game:

- How do your young people approach difficult tasks?

- Is whistling a dying art?

- How important is being able to clearly communicate your message?

- How do you respond to an unclear message yourself?

55. Cereal box game

Theme connection: Flexibility, challenge

Age suitability: 9+

Resources needed: An empty cereal box, a pair of scissors

Venue requirements: None

Background preparation: None

The game

The game centres around the task of picking up the cereal box from the floor, using only the mouth. So far, so easy (try not to think about the saliva issue!). However, the rule is that only feet are allowed to touch the ground; if anything else does, accidentally or intentionally, that person is out.

The best way to play the game is to get the group sitting in a circle with the cereal box in the middle. Go around the circle with each player taking a turn to attempt to pick up the cereal box using their mouth (teeth/lips/whatever). On the first pass round be generous with any who are struggling, and allow multiple attempts if you are the generous sort.

Once everyone has completed the task, take up the scissors and cut off the top 5 cm of the cereal box, leaving it still intact with a flat and attached bottom, but now significantly shorter. Proceed around the circle again, this time eliminating people who fail. At the end of the round cut another strip off the cereal box, and repeat.

Gradually, as you eliminate players, and the top of the box gets closer and closer to the ground, you will discover your remaining players have freakish abilities and bend in ways that you no longer can. Keep going until you have a winner. I have seen the "box" being picked up legitimately when all it consisted of was the flat bottom with no edges/sides left; in which case declare anyone who can do that joint winners. (And then invest in the services of a youth group osteopath.)

What's the purpose?

Possible learning/discussion points from this game:

- Being flexible in life can be a useful skill. How have your young people encountered this?
- Can this cause problems?

56. Cup pick-up

Theme connection: Awareness, challenge

Age suitability: 7+

Resources needed: An empty plastic cup

Venue requirements: A large open space is ideal, but not essential

Background preparation: None

The game

Less of a competitive game, and more of an exercise in skill and memory. Get everyone standing in a circle with a plastic cup (empty) in the middle. Get everyone to look at the cup, and then pick one volunteer to close their eyes and, without opening them, walk forward and pick up the cup. No peeking is allowed, and nor is any vague sweeping of the hands! Allow other people to take a turn. If they develop skills in this area, try using a variety of objects – be inspired by what you have lying around, although round things (like footballs) can present a real challenge.

What's the purpose?

Possible learning/discussion points from this game:

- How aware of their surroundings are your young people?
- How much do they rely on instinct?

57. Yes/No game

Theme connection: Answers, truth

Age suitability: 9+

Resources needed: (Optional water sprayer)

Venue requirements: None

Background preparation: Prepare as many questions as you can

The game

Get two volunteers to stand facing each other, with you as leader in between them. Explain that you will be asking them questions alternately, and that the only rule is their response must not include "yes" or "no".

If you want to use this as a simple illustration at the front, just use two volunteers and see who can last the longest without using "yes" or "no" in a head-to-head competition. Alternatively, if you want to get more people involved ,tell everyone to queue up, and as soon as one of your players uses a "yes" or "no" response, replace them with the next person in the queue.

For added youth work payback/joy, use a water sprayer (the kind you'd use on houseplants) to squirt your participants in the face every time they use yes/no, or if they take too long answering a question.

Tips: Use a real variety of questions; switch quickly between the competitors to deny them time to pause and think; follow threads of questions through with each competitor, and then confuse them by asking a question which connects to their rival's questions; if anyone is doing too well, ask them a couple of questions in succession which don't have a potential yes/no response, before suckering them with a quick yes/no question (e.g. "Who do you think is the greatest footballer ever?" "Which football team do you support?" "Who's the worst manager in the league?" "Would you want their job?").

What's the purpose?

Possible learning/discussion points from this game:

- This could lead into an open discussion on truthfulness.

- Peter writes that we should be prepared to give a reason "for the hope that is in you" (1 Peter 3:15). Are your group ready to do this?

58. Jelly Baby Apocalypse

Theme connection: Sin

Age suitability: 11+

Resources needed: A bag of Jelly Babies

Venue requirements: None

Background preparation: Some jelly sweets are not suitable for vegetarians, so either use a brand that are or ensure that your volunteers are aware of this

The game

This is a two player game that works best as an upfront game, either as a personal challenge, or with representatives from two teams competing in front of the group. As well as the Jelly Babies, all you need are two people who are willing to get a bit sticky for Jesus (or at least for a game). Explain that the basis of the competition is to see who can stick the most Jelly Babies to their own face.

Toss a coin to see which player goes first, and then pass the first sweet to the starting player. They have to bite the head off the unfortunate innocent confectionery, and then stick the remaining part of the Jelly Baby to their face. Play then passes to their opponent who has to do likewise. Play passes between the two competitors to find the person who is able to stick the most Jelly Babies on their visage!

If you had a lot of sweets and a small enough group, you could play this as a game where everyone plays simultaneously, eliminating those who failed to stick a new Jelly Baby to their face at the end of each round.

What's the purpose?

Possible learning/discussion points from this game:

- You could compare this game to the "stickiness" of sin and talk about being set free from sin by Jesus.

- People often joke about being squeamish at biting the heads off Jelly Babies – why do your group think they might do this?

59. Who's in the box?

Theme connection: Identity, community, judgment

Age suitability: 7+

Resources needed: A large empty box

Venue requirements: None

Background preparation: Secretly hide one of your leaders (or more responsible young people) in the box without the rest of the group knowing who's there. You will need to ensure that the group can't simply identify who it is by working out who's missing, so perhaps set it up so that there are a number of individuals who aren't in the room at the time the game is played, although also don't make explicit that it's one of the leaders in the box

The game

Reveal the box to your group and explain that they have to try to work out who's in the box by asking a series of questions, to which the person in the box answers by knocking on the wall of the box – once for yes, twice for no. Get the group to take it in turns to ask questions, ensuring that the questions are vague and related to likes/dislikes rather than being too specific about appearance and so on.

You could try repeating this on successive weeks with different people in the box, or even over the course of the same evening if you have space/opportunity to secretly place other people in the box of mystery.

What's the purpose?

Possible learning/discussion points from this game:

- How do you know what someone is really like?

- Do you ever find yourself judging by appearances?

60. What's in the blender?

Theme connection: Mixing things up, judgment

Age suitability: 7+

Resources needed: A variety of foodstuffs and drinks, a blender, enough cups for everybody

Venue requirements: None

Background preparation: Collect a number of food and drink items that wouldn't usually be coupled together, and blend them until an inevitably yucky and grey drink or paste is produced. (Make sure you include at least one item that is mainly liquid based to allow for it to bind together.) Check any allergies in your group.

The game

Produce your blended concoction and pour some into a cup for each of your group to sample. Give them each a piece of paper and a pen and explain that they need to try to identify what went into the blender. Tell them how many ingredients they are trying to identify, but don't give them any more hints unless they are really stuck.

A variant you could try if you have enough blenders is to produce a number of different blends (minimum three) but tell your group all of the various ingredients, and get them to work out which went into which blend.

Make sure beforehand that you are aware of any allergies, and that what you choose to blend is suitable for all those who will be consuming it!

What's the purpose?

Possible learning/discussion points from this game:

- The OT has plenty of rules that relate to purity and mixing things, (how) is this relevant to your life?

- Did these things taste different to how they looked? Do we sometimes judge too much by appearances?

61. Tangle tunnel

Theme connection: Solving problems, teamwork

Age suitability: 9+

Resources needed: None

Venue requirements: None

Background preparation: None

The game

Divide your group into teams of six to eight (if numbers allow) before building up to doing this with the whole group together in one line. To start off with, get each team into a queue-like line with each person facing the back of the person in front of them. Get each person to place their left hand between their legs, reaching backwards, and then with their right hand to grasp the left hand of the person in front of them. (The person at the front will obviously have their right hand free, and the person at the back will have their left hand free likewise.)

The goal is for the line to untangle themselves without letting go of hands, or lifting their feet over the chain. In effect, then, the back person has to crawl through the legs of the people in front of them, and as they pass through each person's legs that person then has to follow on in order to avoid letting go and breaking the chain. Eventually, when everyone has crawled through, the line should be untangled. Build up to doing it in one line with the whole group.

What's the purpose?

Possible learning/discussion points from this game:

- Do you enjoy solving or untangling issues/problems?

- Do you feel connected to the people around you in life?

- Do you think the problems/challenges of others impact on you?

62. Blindfold taste test

Theme connection: Identity, culture

Age suitability: 7+

Resources needed: Foods from a variety of countries/cultures, blindfolds for everybody, plates and cutlery

Venue requirements: None

Background preparation: Identify about half a dozen countries and their representative foods. For example, Germany could be some form of spicy bratwurst, Mexico might be tacos, Japan could be sushi, for Greece try baklava, the USA can be burgers, Switzerland might be Toblerone. Five minutes of Googling will provide plenty of ideas better than these – don't be afraid of being stereotypical in order for this game to work best! Then find sufficient quantities of these foods to allow your group to each try a bit, as well as providing each member of your group with a blindfold and complete list of the countries included, plus some red herrings. (Do not include actual red herrings, as it could a) potentially make your meeting space smell for a long time, and b) allow for a lot of confusion relating to various Scandinavian nations.)

The game

Explain to your group that this is a blindfold taste test where once everyone is blindfolded, each player will be given a bite-size portion of a food from one of the countries. Once they have eaten it, they have to mark on their list of countries which one they think that food represented. Get them all seated at tables, and make sure blindfolds are on before putting a sample of each food in front of each player (with or without cutlery, depending on the messiness of the food/how bothered you can be to wash up 120 teaspoons). Allow them to take their blindfolds off in between each "course" to mark their selection on the list of countries, but make sure everyone is blindfolded again before bringing out the next selection of cuisine.

At the end announce what the correct countries and food pairings were, and see who got the most correct answers.

What's the purpose?

Possible learning/discussion points from this game:

- How comfortable are you with foreign cultures?

- Do you feel familiar with things that are "different"?

- Do you think God cares about countries and national boundaries – or would he rather we were all just one?

4

Big and Memorable

I don't remember a single teaching point from my time as a teenager in a Christian youth group. Despite the many hours of prep and prayer which my leaders will undoubtedly have put in each week, I couldn't honestly tell you one thing I learned in that group. There are, however, two things which I *do* remember, and they're linked. The first was the fact that our leaders really cared about us, really liked us, and dedicated themselves to our flourishing. The second was an illustration of that first point: the effort that they put into making our group's activities the best they could be.

There was the legendary night hike, which I think I'm still recovering from twenty years later. There were the Safari suppers (a youth group staple of the 1980s and 1990s), where we'd eat our own body weight travelling around the houses of enthusiastic church members, all of whom had over-catered. More regularly, though, there were the games. And while some of them were the predictable things we used to play before the age of risk assessments, others were huge events. One leader in particular used to spend much of his week planning these complex operations, often involving home-made Heath Robinson contraptions and huge amounts of messy food.

> *My experiences are fairly similar actually (maybe there's something in this? ooh...). The midnight hike that led to being stuck on the steep sides of a river valley with nothing but a sheer slope down to the fast-flowing waters in the pitch black of night... Good times. (Side track: do you think that youth leaders in the "good*

old days" had fewer worries about risk?) They were certainly memorable, though. And definitely the kind of "big" experience that led to really good relationships between us as youth and the leader!

The following games might not quite be on the scale of the death-defying night hike, but in most cases they will demand a fair amount of work from you if they're going to be done right. Please, don't let that put you off. That sense of awe and wonder they can generate is a rare thing these days, and has the power to make the bigger stuff you're trying to communicate – like the fact that they're loved by you and by God – stick in their heads for the long-term.

63. Cotton Bud Wars

Theme connection: War

Age suitability: 11+

Resources needed: Lots of straws (ideally ones with bendy necks, as this allows for "aiming"), a plentiful supply of cotton buds (minimum twenty to thirty per player), stuff for barricades (tables/chairs/boxes, etc.)

Venue requirements: A large (ish) space

Background preparation: Divide your playing area in half, marking out a HQ section of about a metre square in each half

The game

Split your group into two teams, and explain that you're going to have a cotton bud war in which their task is to fire as many cotton buds as possible into their opponents' territory, and ideally into the HQ section, while simultaneously trying to keep their territory clear of any cotton buds fired in by the opposition. Explain that their team will score minus ten points for each cotton bud that lands within their HQ, and minus five points for each of their own cotton buds found within their territory at the end of the battle. Make clear that while they are not allowed to touch any cotton buds that do land in their HQ zone, they can however pick up and return fire with any cotton buds that land in the rest of their territory.

Before you start give each team an equal number of whatever your venue has lying around in plentiful supply (e.g. chairs/tables/kneelers, etc.) and allow two minutes for them to create some form of barricade to protect their territory and their HQ. Once this is done, explain that each battle in the war lasts three minutes, hand out the straws and equal supplies of cotton buds, and let hostilities commence.

At the end of the three minutes sound the ceasefire, and send each team into opposing territory to gather and count all the cotton buds lying about. Tally the scores up before sending the teams back into their territories with two minutes to make any changes to their barricades before dividing out the cotton buds for another round.

You will need to consider the safety aspect of firing cotton buds around and the risk of one going into an eye – a creative solution would be to sweet-talk someone in the chemistry department of any local school and see if you can borrow a collection of safety goggles. Alternatively, accumulate a collection of sunglasses and ensure that each participant wears a pair of glasses during the game. (There is some genuine comedic potential in this solution!)

If you have larger groups/more space, you could think about having more teams (up to four). In this case, before beginning get each team to mark an identifying colour on each of their cotton buds so that points can be correctly attributed to the right teams. In this scenario care will need to be taken to ensure that each territory is equally accessible to the other teams' artillery.

What's the purpose?

Possible learning/discussion points from this game:

- Is warfare always pointless?

- Is the doctrine of a "just war" useful?

64. Trusted voices

Theme connection: Listening to God, discernment, trust

Age suitability: 11+

Resources needed: Blindfolds, various large but safe obstacles

Venue requirements: You will need a venue with space for a safe obstacle course – meaning plenty of floor space and nowhere where a blindfolded young person might bang their head or trip over into something dangerous! If space doesn't allow, you could transfer this game outside, but only if the external space is relatively quiet. This won't work next to a busy road

Background preparation: Set up an obstacle course in your venue. The course should be fairly tricky, but crucially should be made from soft, harmless objects that won't cause too many trips

The game

Blindfold a volunteer, and set them at the start of the course, out of earshot of the rest of the group. Now choose another volunteer to be their trusted guide. This person is going to direct the blindfolded young person safely around the course by calling out clear instructions.

But there's a twist. Choose another two volunteers. These people will also try to direct the blindfolded young person, but their role is to misdirect them, send them off to the wrong end of the course, and cause them to bump into various obstacles.

To make it more devious, these three young people are all only allowed to speak one sentence at a time, and have to do so in order: so the trusted voice goes first, followed by the first liar, then the second, followed by the trusted voice again, and so on.

Do not explain what is going on to the blindfolded young person – only say that members of the group are going to guide him to the end of the course. Now the three voices must compete to convince him that theirs is the voice that can be trusted.

What's the purpose?

Possible learning/discussion points from this game:

- We need to learn who we can trust. Primarily we know we can trust God, but there are also friends along the journey who we learn to trust, as well as people that we realize we can't or shouldn't...

- Part of Christian maturity is learning to discern the voice of God. In our culture there are so many competing voices trying to get our attention – in the media, online, and in our everyday life. Hearing God's voice above all this noise is a skill we learn – it doesn't come naturally to most of us.

65. Irate Avians (cough)

Theme connection: Building, war

Age suitability: 9+

Resources needed: Anything that can be used to construct "barriers" – a couple of tables and chairs would suffice, but anything more creative would be great (boxes/kneelers/beanbags). Foam balls. A catapult (e.g. two bungees, or an old jumper stretched out by its arms, held between two leaders). Hats (optional)

Venue requirements: A large space

Background preparation: Gather your construction materials into your playing space

The game

Divide your group into two teams and nominate one team as the team of birds and the other as the naughty pigs. (If none of this makes sense, Google "Angry Birds", or get a young person to explain it!)

Explain that the birds need to defeat the pigs by firing foam balls to hit them, while the pigs need to have constructed some form of barriers to make that difficult. Allow them whatever resources you have available – chairs and a couple of tables on their sides should be adequate – but explain that once a ball touches the item it will be removed by the leaders, and anything that is supported by it is also counted as being destroyed and removed. They also need to be aware that the ball remains "live" until it stops rolling, and rebounds are allowed. If a pig is touched by the ball they are out (although you can allow one or two per team to be pigs in hats which require two hits for removal; offer some suitably silly headgear to identify these). You'll need a couple of leaders to be on removal duty – keeping an eye on what the ball touches and removing it all once the ball stops moving. Gradually the birds will uncover the pigs and hopefully begin to remove them from the playing arena.

Come up with whatever creative ways you like of firing the foam balls (a couple of bungees twisted together and held between two people works well, but if you don't have access to this, an old jumper stretched out in a similar way makes a good catapult) but make sure you give the teams enough time to practise – a couple of minutes while the pigs are setting up their barriers should suffice.

Keep track of how many shots the birds take to eliminate the pigs. Once they have done this, swap roles, giving the new pigs the same time and resources to build their barriers.

What's the purpose?

Possible learning/discussion points from this game:

- Is it more fun to create or destroy? Why do you think this is?

- Do you ever feel "under attack"?

66. Veggielympics!

Theme connection: Sport, food, celebration

Age suitability: 11+

Resources needed: Brussels sprouts, celery, turnips, swedes, string, large table

Venue requirements: You'll need a large clear table or similar, ideally indoors for the sprout blowing element – the other two parts will probably work better outside

Background preparation: Set up the course for the three elements of the game in advance. You could really go to town with this, setting up Olympic flags around the venue, handing out running vests, and so on

The game

Health and safety best practice suggests that Chubby Bunnies is no longer a recommended youth ministry activity, so instead pull volunteers out of the group to compete against one another in the following food-based events:

Celery javelin

Recreate the thrills and spills of the Olympics by seeing who can throw a stick of celery the furthest. Make sure your competitors use the traditional javelin technique, and include a false start line (made of string) to stop any cheating. You may have some in the group who can throw a long way – so this might work best outside.

Sprout-blowing dash

On a table, use string to create two "lanes", then get two volunteers to compete to blow a Brussels sprout to the finish line the fastest. If they blow their sprout out of their lane, they have to go back to the start.

Vegete-boule

Play a quick game of boules using a small round vegetable (e.g. a sprout) as the "jack", and two sets of larger round vegetables (e.g. turnips vs swedes) as the boules. As with the original game, the closest vegetable to the "jack" wins.

Award small chocolate prizes for the victors in each competition, and offer the vegetables to the losers!

What's the purpose?

Possible learning/discussion point from this game:

- Sport is a massive deal for many young people, but we should never lose sight of the sense of fun at the heart of it. It's only a game...

67. Eighties coin-op little yellow man eating things (cough, cough)

Theme connection: Challenge, justice

Age suitability: 9+

Resources needed: Items for maze construction, balloons

Venue requirements: A large hall (enough space to construct a "maze" to run round in)

Background preparation: Construct some form of simple maze (à la the Pac-Man game). Rows of chairs would be ideal for this, or if you're really brave you can just play in church, using the pews! Inflate your balloons (about thirty or so) and dot them around the maze. Clearly mark a number of them as special (perhaps choose a specific colour of balloon).

The game

Divide your group into two teams and allocate one as Team Pac-Man, and the other as Team Ghost. Team Pac-Man's job is to run around the maze without being caught whilst popping as many of the balloons as possible, while Team Ghost has to try to catch the Pac-Men (Pac-People?) before they can pop them all. Explain to the teams that if a Pac-Man is caught (by a ghost tagging them) then a teammate is allowed into the maze to replace them, and that they need to work out what order they will replace each other in. Also explain that if a Pac-Man pops one of the special balloons, then any ghosts in the maze have to freeze in position for ten seconds, during which time they can be tagged by a Pac-Man and then are out and need to be replaced by a teammate in the same way.

Chose three Pac-Men and three Ghosts to start the game, and play until all the balloons are popped or all the Pac-Men have been caught. Then swap the teams' roles over.

What's the purpose?

Possible learning/discussion points from this game:

- We're often told there are enough resources in our world for everyone – do you think this is true?

- Do you feel that you are in competition with anyone/anything?

68. Human Guess-who

Theme connection: Identity, judgment

Age suitability: 11+

Resources needed: Enough chairs for the players to sit on

Venue requirements: A room large enough for a regular grid of chairs

Background preparation: Set out chairs in a regular and even grid pattern (e.g. four rows of four people, etc.)

The game

Get your group to sit on the chairs in a grid, and pick two players to stand in front of them – these players will compete against each other to see who can identify the other person's "pick" in the shortest number of turns.

Instruct the first player to secretly choose one of the group seated in front of them and write their name down so that you, the youth leader, can check there's no sneaky changing of minds going on. Get the entire group to stand up, and then allow the other player to ask "yes"/"no" questions about the person who has been picked. For example: "Is the person male?" "Are they wearing glasses?" "Do they have blonde hair?" "Is the person Danielle?"

After each question they need to instruct the relevant members of the group – those who don't fit the criteria – to sit down to help them see the remaining possibilities.

Record the number of questions taken to identify the correct person, and then swap the roles over to see if their opponent can identify their person in a smaller number of guesses. For those meeting in Nonconformist churches, this game works really well from a balcony!

What's the purpose?

Possible learning/discussion points from this game:

- Do you ever judge based on appearances?

- How important is image to you?

- Do you prefer to conform or to be individual (and is one necessarily "better" than the other)?

69. Lemonade Bowling

Theme connection: Challenge, waste

Age suitability: 7+

Resources needed: A dozen empty two-litre drinks bottles, tables, a football

Venue requirements: A hall long enough for a decent bowling alley

Background preparation: Fill the bottles about a third of the way up with water (any less and it's too easy to knock them over, any more and it's too difficult; experiment to find the optimum fill level for your group). Set them out at one end of your playing area in the ten pin bowling formation (keeping two back as substitutes if any get too battered). Place some tables on their sides to create an alley leading towards the pins, and one across the end as a backboard, remembering to leave gaps between them for the "gutter", and ensuring they aren't so close to the pins that it presents no challenge. Make sure the alley is long enough and mark out a bowling line.

The game

You could play this as a team competition or simply with individuals competing in the manner of a bowling alley. Use the football as a substitute bowling ball.

Allow each competitor (or team) ten goes (or reduce this as appropriate if you have lots of players). Make life easier for yourself and score it simply on the number of bottles knocked over per ball (eliminating any possibly contentious and/or difficult maths to do with the spares and strike system!). Get a team of volunteers to reposition the bottles after each go, and make sure you keep score.

What's the purpose?

Possible learning/discussion points from this game:

- Do you find it easy to set yourself a target and achieve it?

- How do you feel when things go wrong and the ball rolls into the metaphorical gutter of life?

70. Lo-fi paintball

Theme connection: War

Age suitability: 11+

Resources needed: A supply of disposable white painting overalls, non-toxic powder paint, some large buckets, as many water pistols/water bombs as possible

Venue requirements: An outside space

Background preparation: Mix up several buckets of the paint, ideally of at least two different colours, and use it to fill up the water pistols/bombs, ensuring you have an even number per paint colour. Find a large open space (ideally away from other people) and hide a cache of water pistols/bombs for each colour paint you've used. Make sure your young people are aware of what you'll be doing in advance

The game

Give each player a set of overalls and divide them into teams (as many teams as there are different colour paints used), telling them that this is a team game where the aim is to get the opposition more covered in paint than they are. Let them know which colour paint they are representing and roughly where to look for their weapon supplies, and once you've retired to a safe distance let them go for it. Give them a time limit and appoint a leader as unbiased adjudicator of which team is most covered in paint at the end.

Make sure you warn your group in advance to wear old clothes; the coveralls provide some protection but some paint may still get through. It may be worth borrowing sets of safety goggles from the local school science department if possible – alternatively if you want you can get your group to bring their own goggles to protect their eyes.

What's the purpose?

Possible learning/discussion points from this game:

- This game, and other "war"-based games can be immensely fun. Real war obviously isn't. What do you think makes the game versions of war fun?

- What current wars are your group aware of around the world? How aware are they of the reasons behind the conflicts?

71. China Smash

Theme connection: War, destruction, waste

Age suitability: 11+

Resources needed: Old china, old golf balls, tarpaulins

Venue requirements: Outside space, with a high and sturdy wall, and away from passers-by

Background preparation: Collect as much old china as you can (chipped/damaged/hideous ornaments – it's worth contacting local charity shops for any unsaleable items, or offering to take any unsold stock from church fetes). Also gather a supply of old golf balls (again using whatever contacts you have in the community – perhaps the local golf course has a supply of old balls, or local charity shops might be able to help) and get some tough tarpaulins together. At your suitable outside space, set the tarpaulins out on the ground and to protect the wall. Set up the china on something like an old bookshelf or old chairs (whatever is available) to create a "display" of hopefully old china plates/ mugs/bowls and assorted ornaments. Mark out a safe exclusion zone (about twenty to twenty-five feet should be safe) and make sure that the tarpaulins cover the ground where shards of china could land – this makes clearing up easier as well as making sure you don't leave any potentially dangerous litter. Mark out the throwing line. <u>Carefully risk assess this for your group.</u>

The game

Let your group line up one at a time behind the line to throw the golf balls and smash the china, getting leaders to (carefully) return the golf balls and restock the china when necessary. Whether this activity lasts for ages or is over quite quickly is dependent on your stock of china – this will run out long before the enthusiasm of your group for breaking things! Safety is, of course, of paramount importance here – make sure you have enough space to be able to do this activity safely and that your group understand the safety issues.

What's the purpose?

Possible learning/discussion points from this game:

- How do you feel when you see a carefully constructed and possibly much loved ornament shatter?

- Why is breaking something such a fun activity?

- Can something as destructive as war ever achieve anything positive?

72. Silly-lympics

Theme connection: Honesty, justice, sport

Age suitability: 9+

Resources needed: Some or all of the following: rope, paper plates, pens, cotton wool balls, matchboxes, tape measure, coins, etc.

Venue requirements: A hall

Background preparation: Dependent on which events you choose to run

The game

Rather than one game, this is a compilation of games that can create one memorable session's worth of activity. Run it as a collection of individual events, allowing your young people to sign up to whichever ones interest them, and allocating points for competing (e.g. ten), and the top three in each "discipline" (e.g. 1st – 100, 2nd – 75, 3rd – 50). Then at the end of the session add up the total points and announce your silly-lympics champion. For the team events (matchbox racing, tug of war, rowing regatta) award the team's score to each individual on that team.

Tug of war

Get a long rope (ensuring it's strong enough to bear the weight of your teams) and divide your competitors into teams. Mark out two lines, and get the teams to line up at one of these each, holding the rope between them. Mark the middle of the rope, and the winner is the first team to pull that marker to "their" line.

Paper-plate discus

Give each competitor a paper plate, and get them to write their name on it. Put them all standing in a line stretched out along the edge of your throwing space, and on the count of three get them all to throw their plates at the same time (throwing like a Frisbee is probably the best technique). This is a sneaky/lazy way of running the event if you have lots of competitors where measuring each individual throw would be time consuming, as this way you only need to identify the furthest three plates by checking the names written on them. Score it on where the plates end up, not where they land.

Cotton wool shot-put

Give each competitor a ball of cotton wool (available from the baby products aisle at all good supermarkets) and get them lined up as for the paper plate discus game. This time, however, get them to throw one at a time, and note the furthest thrown as you work your way along the line of competitors. The technique for throwing them should be similar to the actual shot-put – a push motion from the shoulders – but make sure none of the more "enterprising" competitors give themselves an advantage by sneakily dampening the cotton wool ball to allow it to fly further!

Matchbox racing

Get a supply of (empty) matchboxes (cheaply available in bulk from supermarkets). Group your competitors into even teams, and split each team into two parts. Send one half of the team to one end of your racetrack, and the other to the other end. Give each team a matchbox and instruct them to push the matchbox across the floor with their noses along the course, from one end to the other in a relay style, until all the team members have had a go. This game will not work on heavily carpeted floors, and do be on the lookout for people cheating by pushing with hair/tongue/chin, etc. Make sure you have some spare matchboxes to replace any that get squashed during the event. For some reason this event, as unpromising as it sounds, is always one of the most eagerly awaited and enjoyed.

Standing jump

Mark out a starting line and, one at a time, get your competitors to stand on it, with both feet firmly planted. On the command they need to jump as far forward as they can, landing upright on both feet. Measure the distance from the line to the back of the heels.

Rowing regatta

The rowing segment can be done as an individual race, or as a team race. The basic premise is that, sitting on the floor, the competitors need to propel themselves backwards by drawing their knees to their chin and then pushing themselves back with their legs. If done as an individual race, just get your competitors lined up at the start of your course (an oval track with chairs marking out the course works well), or if as a team event, get the team seated in a line and add the rule that they have to hold onto the waist of the teammate seated in front of them at all times. (This race is also a good way to get your hall floor polished...)

Chair against the wall

An endurance event. Find enough flat wall space to allow all your competitors to do this simultaneously. Get them to "sit" against the wall, with legs bent 90° at the knees, back straight against the wall, and with no other support allowed. The winners are the people who can maintain this stance the longest without falling to the ground screaming.

Coin spin marathon

Collect as many two pence pieces as you can, and present your competitors (one at a time) with an empty tabletop (or other suitable hard surface) and as many coins as they need – and give them thirty seconds to get as many coins spinning simultaneously as they can.

What's the purpose?

Possible learning/discussion points from this game:

- Is there such a thing as Olympian spirit?

- What do you think about cheating in sports? How about in life in general?

- What's the difference between cheating and "just doing what you can to get ahead"?

73. Fight boats, or Angry Vessels

Theme connection: War, honesty

Age suitability: 11+

Resources needed: Rows of chairs to form a grid

Venue requirements: Two large spaces, each out of sight of the other – e.g. two connected rooms, or one large hall with a large sheet/barricade dividing it

Background preparation: Prepare a grid in each space, using chairs or making on the floor with tape/chalk. As a basic guide try to ensure that the ratio of empty space to players is no more than two to one (i.e. if you have ten players on each team then make the grid thirty spaces in total, so a five by six grid)

The game

Separate your group into two equal teams and send one team to each room. Get them to place themselves on the grid in the manner of battleships. The only rule is that they have to be in "ships" of at least two people – directly next to at least one other person either horizontally or vertically on the grid, as ships are not allowed to go diagonally.

Teams take it in turns to nominate a position on the opposition's grid to shell (number the rows A, B, C... and the columns 1, 2, 3...). If someone is in that space they have to shout "arrrggh, you've got me", and if it's an empty space get everyone on the team to shout "splosh". The winning team is the first to successfully hit all their opposition's ships. Give each team a blank grid on paper to mark out their attempts and remember where they've tried.

Keep the game moving at pace, and make sure that no one moves their position once the game starts.

What's the purpose?

Possible learning/discussion points from this game:

- Discussions on warfare, or the nature of honour in battle, could flow naturally out of this.

- Were either of your groups tempted to cheat?

- How did they feel about the other team once they got "hit"?

74. A-maze-ing fun with boxes

Theme connection: Challenge, being lost

Age suitability: 11+

Resources needed: Many large cardboard boxes, sheets, tables

Venue requirements: Space to create a large maze

Background preparation: Using a combination of boxes that are open at both ends (creating tunnels) and boxes that open at one end only (creating dead ends), and creatively taping them together to create T-junctions, tunnels, blind alleys, and multiple junctions, you can construct a maze of limitless potential. Start by lying some tables on their sides to make the outer walls of your maze (remembering to leave space for an entrance and exit!), and then simply begin positioning your boxes within. Once you're happy with your layout, drape some sheets over the top of the boxes and tables to add a roof and make the maze more challenging, taping the sheets themselves together and to the tables to allow some structural integrity.

The game

Once you've made your maze you can use it in a number of ways. If you have set it up so that there is an entrance and exit, and a sufficiently complex pathway through, you can simply time your young people to see how long it takes them to negotiate the maze.

Or, if you are feeling more creative and are agile enough to get round the maze yourself, you could hide letters on pieces of paper around the maze and send young people in one at a time to bring out one piece of paper each. They then need to work together to put the letters in order and spell out some message or word.

What's the purpose?

Possible learning/discussion points from this game:

- What's it like to feel lost or trapped?

- How do you find your way out of a tricky situation?

75. Time-bomb

Theme connection: Self-control, greed, consumerism

Age suitability: 11+

Resources needed: A series of increasingly delicious treats, starting with a sweet, and moving up through small chocolate bars to an amazing slab of cake or chocolate; large box to disguise these; the "boing" recording (see below)

Venue requirements: None

Background preparation: Make a recording (how you do this will depend on how technologically savvy you're feeling) of a ticking clock. At a point determined by you (I would suggest between forty-five and sixty seconds in), add a loud klaxon, buzzer, or "boing" sound effect. If you want to play the game several times, make several different recordings, putting the "boing" in different places in each one (including one where it goes off almost straight away). Before you start, write out your running order of treats for your own ease. For instance: boiled sweet, fun-size chocolate bar, jelly beans, doughnut, full-size chocolate bar, large chocolate bar... slab of cake

The game

Ask for a volunteer with a sweet tooth. Explain that you're going to reach into your box, and retrieve a series of treats. When they see the one they want to take and eat, they can shout "stop", and it's theirs. The thing is, the treats keep getting better.

But there's a twist! While you're doing this, a ticking time-bomb will be getting ready to explode. At any point, the ticking noise they're about to hear will be punctuated by an explosion, and if that happens, they get nothing! So the aim of the game is to get away with the best treat they can without losing out.

You may want to create several recordings, in order to play the game several times. If the person shouts "stop" early, give them their treat, then run the recording as you would have done, continuing to offer them treats at the same pace – although now they're stuck with the treat they chose. If they went for the jelly beans, be prepared for them to be quite disappointed!

What's the purpose?

Possible learning/discussion points from this game:

- Sometimes we can get greedy – and this can blow up in our faces.

- One of the most important skills a Christian can learn – and a fruit of the Spirit – is self-control. It means that we master our desires, instead of letting them master us.

76. Multi-ball non-stop box-wall volleyball

Theme connection: Challenge, solving problems

Age suitability: 11+

Resources needed: Boxes

Venue requirements: A hall large (and high) enough to play volleyball

Background preparation: Build a wall of boxes in the place of a volleyball net, as tall as a normal net if possible

The game

Divide your group into two teams, and send each team to one half of your hall. Explain that you are going to play "multi-ball non-stop box-wall volleyball". (A very satisfying name to say, try it!) Played similarly to normal volleyball (where the aim is to prevent the ball from touching the ground by hitting it over the net into the opponents' court), the key difference is in the scoring system.

In addition to normal scoring (where Team A score a point if the ball lands in Team B's court, or if Team B fail to return the ball over the net), there are also box-related penalties if a team knocks boxes out of the wall. If Team B hits the ball into the wall and no boxes fall, the point simply goes as normal to Team A. However, if any boxes fall out of the wall, then Team A also score a bonus of ten points per box. Similarly, if a player knocks into the wall and dislodges any boxes, again the opposition score a bonus of ten points per box that hits the ground. When a box is dislodged from the wall, simply remove it from the court and continue the game. To speed the game up, whenever points are scored simply restart the game by the nearest person hitting the ball over the net, regardless of team/score, etc.

Continue the game non-stop until either all the boxes are gone or one team reaches 100 points. Play with one ball until your teams have got the grasp of it, then introduce a second ball for simultaneous multi-ball chaos.

What's the purpose?

Possible learning/discussion point from this game:

- What's your approach to obstacles or obstructions in life? Would you rather go round them, clear them away, or try to barge through them?

77. The Christian Maze

Theme connection: Teamwork

Age suitability: 11+

Resources needed: Football (plus extra smaller balls), goalposts, three samples of pureed foods, two bricks, a plank, boxes, sheets, tables, sheets of paper with letters on them (e.g. R.E.V.E.L.A.T.I.O.N.), five boxes with holes cut in them, bag of flour, tomato, cheese, slice of ham, piece of pineapple, video games console, ten general knowledge questions, balloons with pieces of coloured paper inside, stopwatch, whistle, enough "crystals" for each team to win one at the end of each game (though that success rate is unlikely), prizes

Venue requirements: Multiple rooms, including a large set-aside final arena

Background preparation: Set up the different games in distinct as possible areas around your meeting space, and ensure you have enough volunteers to head up each "station"

The game

Based on the popular 1990s TV show, the key to this event is having a number of suitable small games. The following are ideas only, and can simply be substituted for your own "speciality" events.

If your group is large, divide them into teams of five to seven, and start them off each at a different game station. However, this works just as well if your group is small enough that you might want them in smaller teams of three or four, and just have a few games running simultaneously. Ideally, each game should take roughly the same amount of time to complete, so all the "teams" can move round simultaneously.

Station One: Beat the Goalie

Multi-ball chaos. Instruct the team that they need to take it in turns to take penalties past your volunteer. Give them two minutes to attempt to score fifty, and appoint someone reliable to keep count and track of time. It's worth having several balls to remove unnecessary delays in ball-return. (They don't all have to be football-sized, just to make it easier/trickier.) If they score fifty goals within the time they win a crystal. (You can set the target higher or lower depending on the ability of your goalkeeper or age/skill level of your teams.)

Station Two: Name that Food

Get each team to nominate one team member to be the taster, and provide them with three different samples of pureed food. They have to describe the tastes to their teammates who have to try to correctly identify what the puree is. You can use jars of baby food for this, or simply blend together a cooked meal (e.g. fish fingers, chips, peas, and ketchup). The team has to correctly identify all three dishes to win a crystal. You can require them to be as specific as you like.

Station Three: Lava Floor

Introduce the team to an empty room, with two areas marked out either end, and explain that they need to get the whole team from one area to the other without touching the floor. Provide them with two bricks and a plank (or equivalent) to aid them in their task. They only win a crystal if the whole team gets across.

Station Four: Mazey-mess

Create a simple covered maze using tables/boxes and blankets. Make it big enough that your young people can (safely!) crawl about inside. Hide inside it a number of pieces of paper, each with a letter written on it. Instruct the team to go in one at a time, to try to find a letter which they then need to bring out to their teammates. When all the letters have been found, the team needs to rearrange them to spell out a word (e.g. REVELATION). Ensure that there are enough bits of paper for everyone to have a go at finding one in the maze. If they do this correctly within the time limit, they win a crystal.

Station Five: What's in the Box?

Get five large boxes, and cut a hole in the side of each one. Inside each box place one item that is linked to all the others. Get the team to nominate one team member who has to reach through the hole in the box and feel the item inside it, and without looking at it, describe it to their teammates. As a team they then need to identify the link between the five items to get a crystal. So for example you could put in a bag of flour, a tomato, a lump of cheese, a slice of ham, and a bit of pineapple – and they would have to guess Hawaiian pizza (or just pizza if you were feeling kinder!).

Station Six: Beat the Pro

Dependent on your volunteers, you may have one who is particularly good at one of the activities you often have in your youth group (e.g. playing FIFA on the Xbox, or perhaps tennis on the Wii, or table tennis IRL, etc.). Make this station a challenge to beat your volunteer at an activity at which they are expert. The team has to nominate a representative to compete against the expert, and if they beat them, they win a crystal.

Station Seven: General Knowledge Round

Pick your smartest (!) leader to compile a list of ten general knowledge questions, and turn them into your quizmaster. When they reach this station the team has to pick three numbers between one and ten, and the quizmaster reads them the appropriate questions from the list. The team then has to correctly answer all three questions (first answers only) to win a crystal. Only reveal after all three questions have been answered whether they have been answered correctly.

Final challenge: The Christian Dome

In a final set-aside area blow up as many balloons as possible in advance, putting inside each one pieces of paper of two different colours (gold and silver if your stationery budget allows, white and yellow if it doesn't!).

Gather all the teams together and after revealing how many crystals each team has won, explain that each crystal represents five seconds of time inside the balloon pit, where they have to pop the balloons, and collect as many gold pieces of paper, and as few silver pieces, as possible before time runs out.

Explain that each team will be allowed to join in with the appropriate amount of time left as crystals won – so a team with all seven crystals gets the full thirty-five seconds, a team with six gets to join them after five seconds, a team with just four crystals can join in once there are twenty seconds left, etc… Give each team a container into which they need to place their collected bits of paper (put them in different corners of the room to remove confusion) and clarify that there is no stealing of paper allowed, but that any bits on the floor are fair game regardless of who popped the balloon!

Get the teams into their respective corners, and blow a whistle to indicate that the first team can begin popping. Blow the whistle every five seconds, and ensure that each team joins in as appropriate. At the end count up how many pieces of gold paper each team has collected, minus each piece of silver paper, and award prizes based on this.

What's the purpose?

Possible learning/discussion point from this game:

- Do you prefer working as a team or on your own? What are the advantages/disadvantages of each?

78. Treasure hunt relay

Theme connection: Discovery, value

Age suitability: 11+

Resources needed: A pile of random "junk"

Venue requirements: Space to hide objects, preferably more than one room

Background preparation: Hide a number of specific items in advance around your venue, ensuring that you have the right number of objects for the number of teams you anticipate having. For example, if one of the items you will instruct them to find is an inflatable banana, make sure that you have hidden one inflatable banana per team, so each team will be able to search for and find the same list of items

The game

From the name you might surmise that this is a form of a relay race, crossed with a treasure hunt, and you would be right. With your group divided into teams, one at a time you give the team members specific items to find that you have hidden in advance around your meeting venue.

Divide your group into teams dependent on space/number of objects you have hidden, probably in teams of about half a dozen, but crucially ensuring that each team member will have at least one item to find. Explain that it is a team race, and that one at a time team members will be told the name of an item to try to find, and bring back to you as leader. Only once they have done so will you tell the next team member their item to find and so on until the team have completed the list. The first team to find and bring all their items to you wins.

Make sure that the items are scattered around the place and not clumped together (i.e. if one of the items you're making them look for is a rubber chicken, ensure that they are hidden in a variety of locations) and try to make the items that they are looking for as unusual and out of context as possible.

What's the purpose?

Possible learning/discussion points from this game:

- What do you value the most?

- If your heart is where your treasure is (Matthew 6:21), where is your heart?

79. Paper kings

Theme connection: War, Bible

Age suitability: 11+

Resources needed: Lots and lots of newspaper, sticky tape, bin liners

Venue requirements: Ideally this game is played in a big hall, and in a venue that is easy to sweep up in afterwards!

Background preparation: This game is a lot of fun but could create behavioural issues if you select the wrong people as the key volunteers. Be wise in who you choose for the central roles, and make sure everyone is briefed on the rules of engagement – to keep it fun, rather than violent

The game

Divide into either two or four teams – call them "tribes". In each team, appoint one person to be the "warrior king" for that tribe – the rest of the team are now his or her "armour bearers".

Hand out lots – and I mean lots – of newspaper. The teams now have five minutes to completely cover their king with newspaper armour. One important rule here – as part of this, the king must have his or her right arm secured to their body. They are not allowed to use their right arm in this game.

Once your preparation time has elapsed, send your kings into battle in the middle of the room. Their objective is to tear as much newspaper off of their opponents as possible using their left arms only, while protecting their own armour. After one minute, stop the battle, and send the kings back to their armour bearers for another minute of repairs. A king is out once all their armour has been removed.

The game ends either when there is one king left, or when you stop it, and pronounce the king with the most intact armour to be the winner.

What's the purpose?

Possible learning/discussion points from this game:

- The Old Testament is full of war stories – and we can find them difficult to understand, especially in the light of the New Testament, which seems to centre around a pacifist who blessed peacemakers.

- The Israelite army went into battle with God on their side – the equivalent of fighting with two arms against men who could only use one. That's why Gideon's 300 defeated a huge army of hundreds of thousands.

80. Balloon versus Toothpick

Theme connection: Teamwork

Age suitability: 7+

Resources needed: An equal supply of two colours of balloons, the more the better. Enough toothpicks for one per player. Large bin liners

Venue requirements: None

Background preparation: Inflate and tie off the balloons, separating the colours into large bin liners. You should be aware of any young people who might be sensitive to popping balloons, and create a safe space for them during this game.

The game

Divide your group into two teams, and give each team member a toothpick. Explain to them that the age-old battle between inflatable objects and pointy objects is to be settled finally there and then, and that you will be holding a contest to see which team can be first to pop all of their coloured balloons using only their toothpicks. (This isn't as easy as it sounds initially!) Give each team a specific colour of balloon that they need to try to pop, scatter all the balloons across your meeting space, step back, put your earplugs in, and start the contest.

The losing team has to help pick up all the shards of popped balloon that will litter your otherwise immaculate meeting area.

What's the purpose?

Possible learning/discussion points from this game:

- You could use this as a discussion starter about teamwork, and ask the teams whether any of them discovered that working together made it easier.

- Can they think of any situations in life where things that initially seem easy turn out to be difficult?

81. Spider's web

Theme connection: Teamwork, overcoming difficulties, challenge, leadership

Age suitability: 9+

Resources needed: Wool or string, something to attach these to a doorway or frame

Venue requirements: A suitable doorway, or enough space to erect a frame

Background preparation: Tie a series of threads of wool/string across some form of passageway (perhaps a doorway, though probably not a fire escape!) at differing heights and angles – leaving enough spaces between them to fit a body through

The game

Explain to your group that their task is to get the whole team through the door, without touching any of the threads and with the rule that each "gap" can only be used by the team once.

Encourage them to think and discuss how they might help each other get through. If any of the team touch a thread explain that they have awakened some form of giant spider and have to start over again from the beginning.

If time/space/resources allow you could construct a 3D form of this – a larger frame helps in this.

As ever, if an element of competitiveness would aid your group in completing the task, you could time how long it takes each team to fulfil the task requirements – but the real challenge in this task is completing it as a team, and not being "better at it" than anyone else.

What's the purpose?

Possible learning/discussion points from this game:

- Was it easy to work together as a team?

- How did they decide as a team what would happen and in what order?

- Did anyone take on the role of leader? Do people always need a leader?

5

Bible Games

The Bible is fun. All right, perhaps for some people that feels like a slight exaggeration, but if it's not quite fun then it certainly doesn't have to be arduous. Despite some of its more negative cultural connotations, young people don't have to think of it as a boring book about dead people, or as that thing you have to read if you're going to be a good Christian. As youth leaders, it's up to us to show them that there's life, and enjoyment, and wonder, and relevance to their own lives to be found within those pages.

That begins with us discovering it for ourselves, of course. If you're not passionate and excited about the Bible, there's no way that you'll encourage young people to be. Beyond that, though, the way that we address and handle the Bible in our youth groups can have a big impact on how they feel about it. That's what this section is all about.

> It might feel slightly sacrilegious that we're suggesting that your group "play games" involving the Bible – but relax (please!). This isn't about taking the Bible lightly, but about finding ways of getting your group to engage with it. Think of this as a way of getting people who might otherwise never pick up the Bible to get used to the Good Book. (Alternatively you could always just read your group some of the stories rarely covered in Sunday school, involving prophets, hair loss, and marauding bears…)

Jimmy makes a good point there (of course); it's hard to overstate how alien and irrelevant the Bible seems to any young person who hasn't grown up in or around church. An ancient book which apparently prohibits some of their favourite things isn't exactly going to fly to the top of their reading lists – at least not without your help in demystifying and introducing it. So in playing games which make use of the Bible, you're gently helping them to realize that it's not weird, mad, or boring to open a copy.

Just as evangelism often requires "pre-evangelism" to lower barriers and pave the way for serious engagement with faith, these games are designed to help young people take their very first steps in a journey that we hope will culminate in a lifelong positive relationship with the Bible. Essentially: if you want to get them to read the Bible, you'll need to help them hold and open it first; these games offer a great mechanism for that.

82. Bible balloon stomp

Theme connection: Bible

Age suitability: 7+

Resources needed: Balloons, printed verse words (see background preparation), a Bible

Venue requirements: A large hall or other indoor area where balloon bursting isn't going to create a noise issue or threaten breakables

Background preparation: This game is ninety per cent preparation. Select the Bible verse which you'd like to look at, or hope to get the young people to memorize, and type it out in a large font. Cut the verse up into either individual words, or pairs of words. On another small piece of paper type out the verse reference (don't cut this up), and on another write the instruction: "Put the words together to make a Bible verse." Now insert the words to the verse, plus the other two pieces of paper, into individual balloons, and inflate these. You should be aware of any young people who might be sensitive to popping balloons, and create a safe space for them during this game.

The game

Distribute the balloons evenly around the room, then tell everyone to stamp on the balloons and retrieve the secret message hidden inside them. Don't say anything else – just wait for them to figure out what they have to do. After a short time, someone should find the instructions, and they'll begin to order the verse.

At first, don't give them a Bible – see if they can create the verse by using either common sense or prior Bible knowledge. If they're struggling, however, give one of the group a Bible, so that they can look up and assemble the verse. Once the words are in the correct order, ask them to read the verse aloud together.

What's the purpose?

Possible learning/discussion point from this game:

* This is a great way to introduce the idea of a memory verse – the practice of learning Scripture by rote. Set everyone the challenge of learning the verse by heart by the time you next meet together.

83. Bible Racing

Theme connection: Bible

Age suitability: 7+ (reading ages up)

Resources needed: Bibles, paper

Venue requirements: A hall, or at least enough space to run in

Background preparation: Write out on individual slips of paper a selection of Bible verses, ensuring you have at least one slip per player

The game

Divide your group into equally sized teams. Put one Bible per team at one end of your meeting space, accompanying it with a leader equipped with a list of the Bible references you've chosen, plus a copy of the accompanying verses. At the other end of the room place one bowl per team, containing the slips of paper with the Bible references on them (enough for the team members to have one each).

Get the teams lined up behind the bowl. Explain that in the manner of a relay race, they have to pick up a slip of paper from the bowl one at a time, run down to the Bibles, find the appropriate reference, and read it or show it to the leader, before returning to the team and allowing the next player their turn.

This can be made more complex and active dependent on your group and/or space limitations. So you could create something akin to an assault course for the players to get through before finding the Bible verse.

Points to be aware of – be careful of any young people who might not be as familiar with the Bible as others, or those for whom reading is a struggle. Make sure no one is left feeling stupid.

What's the purpose?

Possible learning/discussion points from this game:

- Familiarity with the Bible. How well do the young people know the Bible?

- How easy do we make it in churches/youth groups to use the Bible? Does it feel like a bit of a mission to get anything good out of the "Good Book"?

84. Jesus Name Bingo

Theme connection: Jesus

Age suitability: 11+

Resources needed: You need to make simple grids for each young person: a sheet of paper (probably A4) divided into six squares. You'll also need a pen for everyone

Venue requirements: None

Background preparation: Make sure you know what each of the genuine names for Jesus means and where it originates from

The game

Give everyone a grid divided into six squares, and explain that you're going to read out a number of the names that are given for Jesus in the Bible… and a few words and phrases which aren't. The young people should write down six of these names – those which they believe are genuine names or titles given to Jesus in the New Testament. They should write one name in each box.

Read the following list (you can add your own) but mix up the order: Christ, Lord, The Word, Son of David, Lamb of God, Rabbi, Immanuel, Light of the World, Son of Man… and then the fake ones: The Keeper of Souls, Leader of Christians, The Mighty, Jesus-Bethel, Prince of Dreams, Lighthouse, Staff of Moses, Heart of God, Kevin.

Once they've done that, begin reading the correct names, one by one, and get them to cross off their boxes as the correct answers are read. The first person to get six correct answers – and shout BINGO – wins… if no one manages it, give a prize to the person who got the most correct answers.

What's the purpose?

Possible learning/discussion point from this game:

* The Bible uses many different names for Jesus, to illustrate both the different aspects of who he is (e.g. Rabbi) and the different Old Testament prophecies and traditions that he fulfils (e.g. Immanuel).

85. Bible concentration

Theme connection: Bible

Age suitability: 9+

Resources needed: None

Venue requirements: None

Background preparation: None

The game

Get your group sitting in a horseshoe shape. Starting from one side of the gap, go round naming each seat consecutively as a book from the New Testament: so Matthew, Mark, Luke, John, etc… as far as you have players on seats. (This game works best with about a dozen players, so if you need to go beyond Revelation you might struggle anyway!)

Explain carefully that there is no hierarchy of books in the Bible, but in this game there is, and that the aim is to get to sit on one of the top four (gospel) chairs.

The way this game works is that everyone together establishes a rhythm in which the role of "it" is passed about the group, and anyone who breaks this rhythm gets relegated to the lowest chair, with everyone who was "beneath" that position getting to move up a seat, taking on the new identity of the seat they move to.

To create the rhythm the group gets a regular pattern going by everyone slapping their hands on their legs, then clapping them together, then by clicking the fingers on the left hand, then the fingers of the right hand, and repeating ad infinitum. So the pattern goes slap… clap… click… click… slap… clap… etc. (A good starting rhythm is about 110 b.p.m., detailed instruction fans.) Once everyone has got this, and everyone keeps doing this as the game proceeds, then the next step is adding the competitive element.

This is where the identity of seat is important as the "books" take turns to "pass" to another "book" of their choice, in rhythm, over the clicks.

The game always starts with Matthew (as the "top" book) who passes on to another book, that book then passes on to another book, and so on. So while everyone continues doing the slap, clap, click, click, the book who is passing says their name (e.g. Matthew) on the first click, and on the second click the name of the book they are passing to (e.g. Romans) so it would go: slap, clap, "Matthew, Romans". The person on the Romans chair would then have to pass it on without breaking rhythm: slap, clap, "Romans, Luke". Luke would then need to pass on: slap, clap, "Luke, Philemon", etc., always saying their own name on the first click, and the name of the book they are passing to on the second click, and always without breaking the rhythm.

The rules are that if anyone breaks the rhythm they are immediately relegated to the lowest seat in the circle, and whoever had been beneath them moves up one space, adopting the identity (book) of the chair they move to. Additionally if any player attempts to pass back to the book which passed to them originally, they are relegated, or if anyone makes any other kind of mistake, they get sent down (e.g. speaking when they're not "it", failing to maintain the slap, clap, click, click pattern, or if they forget which book they are, etc.). Restart passing again with the person who has moved into the empty seat.

After a bit of practice the rhythm becomes second nature and you can even speed it up to enhance the difficulty. Set a time limit and award prizes to the players in the top four gospel seats when time is up.

What's the purpose?

Possible learning/discussion point from this game:

- Knowing the Bible can become second nature – how well do you know it?

86. Confucius versus Proverbs

Theme connection: Proverbs, wisdom, Bible

Age suitability: 11+

Resources needed: List of "proverbs" (see below), simple scoreboard (optional)

Venue requirements: None

Background preparation: Make sure you know a little bit about the origins of both Confucius (ancient Chinese philosopher) and the biblical proverbs (phrases taken from a book of wisdom, mainly written by the Israelite King, Solomon)

The game

Split the group into two teams, and set up a simple scoreboard with team names at the top. Explain that you're going to read a list of wisdom phrases – the teams need to work out if they're taken from the Bible (Proverbs), or from the writings and teaching of the ancient Chinese philosopher Confucius. Because there are only two possible answers, teams can only score a point when it's their turn; alternate between the two.

Randomize the two lists below as you read them, and ask for a consensus from each team before you accept their final answer (you may need to appoint a team leader). Score correct answers on the scoreboard behind you, and consider awarding a small prize to the team which attributes the most quotes correctly.

Confucius:

"If one cannot teach his own family, it is not possible for him to teach others."

"The better man is modest in his speech but exceeds in his actions."

"Our greatest glory is not in never falling, but in rising every time we fall."

"He who merely knows right principles is not equal to him who loves them."

"We don't yet know about life; how can we know about death?"

Proverbs:

"Whoever robs their father and drives out their mother is a child who brings shame and disgrace." (19:26)

"Whoever listens to a life-giving rebuke will be at home among the wise." (15:31)

"Do not love sleep or you will grow poor; stay awake and you will have food to spare." (20:13)

"Like a bad tooth or a lame foot is reliance on the unfaithful in times of trouble." (25:19)

"Whoever winks with their eye is plotting perversity." (16:30)

What's the purpose?

Possible learning/discussion points from this game:

- We hear lots of "wisdom", especially in the age of social media. But how do we know what's really wise, and what just sounds like wisdom?

- The Bible says that because Solomon asked God for the gift of wisdom, he was the wisest man who ever lived (1 Kings 4:30). Sometimes we don't think of wisdom as a gift – but the Bible suggests it's something we can pray for more of.

87. Bible Number Treasure Hunt

Theme connection: Bible

Age suitability: 11+

Resources needed: A Bible, a pen and paper for each pair of players

Venue requirements: Space for a treasure hunt, plenty of hiding spaces

Background preparation: Identify a dozen or so verses in the Bible which include a number. Write down each reference on a separate piece of paper (making a note of the numbers as you go along!) and hide each piece somewhere around your building (perhaps stick them to the bottom of objects, in drawers, and so on, ensuring that they are tricky but findable).

The game

Divide your group into pairs and equip each pair with a Bible, pen, and paper. Explain that you have hidden twelve Bible references around the building, and that their task is to find each reference, look it up, and add up the total of all numbers in all the verses they find – and the winners will be the first team to come back to you with the correct answer. (If you have hidden them in particularly difficult places, or perhaps have a large space to hunt in, you could offer clues to where each piece of paper is hidden.)

Points to be aware of – be sensitive to any young people for whom numbers are a struggle. Also make sure the pieces of paper with the Bible reference on them are replaced by each pair once they've found the verse. If you are using a large area for your clues, make sure your leaders are well spread out to ensure safety, and to offer any help if groups get stuck.

What's the purpose?

Possible learning/discussion points from this game:

- Numbers in the Bible often have meaning – seven representing completeness, twelve relating to the tribes of Israel, seventy representing a large number, etc. As a group you could look at some examples in a Bible study.

- Do the things referred to in the Bible have any direct connection with the life of the young people in your group?

- Is the Bible full of irrelevant or archaic details? Do any of these details matter?

88. Bible Who's Who

Theme connection: Community, identity, Bible

Age suitability: 7+ (with familiarity with a range of Bible stories)

Resources needed: Dressing up clothes/props

Venue requirements: None

Background preparation: Leaders to dress up, and familiarize themselves with their characters

The game

Get one of your leaders to dress up as a Bible character, with one or two props that indicate their identity (without being too obvious – a stuffed lion if the leader is being Daniel is probably too helpful!).

Divide your group into two teams (such as boys versus girls) who have to identify the character by means of asking questions that your "character" has to answer with only "yes" or "no". Allow the teams to take it in turns asking questions, or taking their go by making a guess. You could use this game to introduce a topic (though obviously don't announce this in advance – as even twelve-year-old boys are clued up enough to connect a new series on King David with the game at the start of the session guessing who the guy with the slingshot and harp is!) or alternately you could have a number of other characters in mind to play other rounds with.

What's the purpose?

Possible learning/discussion points from this game:

- What makes you "you"? Are there things that would make people recognize you wherever you are?

- Do you think of the people in the Bible as being "real" people, like you or me?

89. The Lord's Gargle

Theme connection: Prayer

Age suitability: 11+

Resources needed: Glasses of water, copies of the Lord's Prayer from Matthew 6:9–13, bucket, small chocolate prizes

Venue requirements: It's only water, but make sure you're somewhere that it's OK to spill it, or have it regurgitated from the mouths of young people on to the floor!

Background preparation: None

The game

A simple but fun way to introduce the topic of prayer to young people, which hopefully also demystifies the concept, and can be used to introduce The Lord's Prayer to young people who have perhaps never heard it.

Get a volunteer to the front, and hand them The Lord's Prayer. Ask them to read it to the group. Now hand them a glass of water, and invite them to read it again, but this time, while gargling. See how far they can get – if they lose the water before the end, their turn is over and someone else can have a go.

If anyone gets right to the end, award them a small prize; otherwise give it to the person who got furthest before losing the water. As a fun extension, see if any of the leaders want to have a go…

What's the purpose?

Possible learning/discussion point from this game:

- Prayer – and even this ancient prayer of Jesus – doesn't have to be a serious, religious business. God wants us to enjoy our relationship with him – like a perfect father–child relationship.

90. Mystery Message

Theme connection: Communication, Bible

Age suitability: 9+

Resources needed: Blank paper, glue, a newspaper per team

Venue requirements: None

Background preparation: Pick a Bible verse for your group to use

The game

A simple craft-based race, divide your group into small groups of three or four, and provide each group with a blank piece of paper, ample supplies of glue, and a whole newspaper. Explain to them that you are going to give them a Bible verse which they need to communicate in the time-honoured style of old-fashioned movie criminals by ripping out words and letters from their newspapers and sticking them together to spell out that message, including the reference. You (or another of your leaders) will then judge the winning message based on the speed with which they put the message together, but also on the tidiness of the sticking and presentation, and on the readability of the message!

Make sure that the sentence you give to the teams is sufficiently challenging and unlikely to appear in any of the newspapers as a complete sentence!

What's the purpose?

Possible learning/discussion points from this game:

- Is communicating through printed media still something we need to know how to do?

- What are the best ways to communicate the message of the Bible in today's world?

91. Paper Plane Pigeon post

Theme connection: Communication, teamwork

Age suitability: 11+

Resources needed: A pile of paper and a pen for each player, a Bible per group of three, instructions in sealed and labelled envelopes

Venue requirements: A large playing area, allowing for the throwing of multiple paper aeroplanes

Background preparation: Prepare written instructions for each player, position as per the instructions below, and seal them in the appropriately labelled envelopes

The game

Divide your group into threes, and give each player a pile of paper and a pen. Send one member of each group of three to the far end of the hall, getting them to spread out across the width of it evenly, place one member of each team across the middle of the hall (also evenly spread, matching their teammates at the end of the hall), and get the remaining member of each team to go to the other end of the hall (again matching the spread of their team).

Give each player at the far end of the hall a Bible and explain to everyone that you are going to give the team member at your end of the hall a set of instructions and/or questions which they have to communicate to their teammate at the far end of the hall, who then needs to reply, and so on. Player Two in the middle of the hall, through whom the team's messages have to pass, will also have a set of instructions which they will need to act on before passing the message on. The players are not allowed to speak or mime, and can only communicate via written instructions on paper aeroplanes.

So Player One writes the question on a piece of paper, makes an aeroplane out of it, and throws it to Player Two (in the middle of the hall) who has to carry out their instruction, before passing it on to Player Three at the far end of the hall. They then have to find the answer, write it down, and pass it back (via aeroplane, and passed through Player Two) to Player One, who then can move on to instruction two.

To make matters more tricky, the players aren't allowed to make more than one step to retrieve a paper aeroplane that has been thrown to them, so if the throw is inaccurate, the player who threw it will need to rewrite the message and make a new paper aeroplane.

The winning team is the first where all team members have completed the instructions/questions. You can make up your own set of instructions, and make it as complicated/creative/long as you like, but an example of what might work is below. Put the instructions in sealed envelopes, labelled Player One – Instruction One, Player Two – Instruction Two, etc. and give them to the appropriate players, on the condition that they cannot open the next instruction until they have completed the first one.

Example instructions:

Player One Instruction One: Send this message to Player Two "Find out what activity King David did in…"

Player Two Instruction One: Add the Bible reference: (2 Samuel 6:14) to the message from Player One and pass it on to Player Three.

Player Three Instruction One: Answer the question from Player One and send the answer back via Player Two.

Player One Instruction Two: Send this message to Player Two "Find out what creature is mentioned in…"

Player Two Instruction Two: Add the Bible reference: (Luke 13:34) to the message from Player One and pass it on to Player Three.

Player Three Instruction Two: Answer the question from Player One and send the answer back via Player Two.

Player One Instruction Three: Do the activity from Instruction One, in the style of the creature in Instruction Two and get Player Two to do the same.

Player Two Instruction Three: Do what Player One is telling you to do, and tell Player Three to do the same.

Player Three Instruction Three: Do what Player Two tells you to do.

What's the purpose?

Possible learning/discussion points from this game:

- Life (like this game) is terrifyingly complicated and yet enjoyable at times – discuss how thinking about this makes you feel (!).

- How do you find following instructions?

- Is it easy to work in a team?

6

Energizers

The world is full of big questions. "Why are we here?" "What is life really all about?" And crucially in this context: "what's the difference between an ice-breaker and an energizer?"

While we probably need a bit more room to tackle the first two of those queries, allow us to answer the third. In essence, while they both tend to refer to high-energy group games, an ice-breaker is used at the beginning of a session to help defuse awkwardness and unfamiliarity, and an energizer is used mid-session to breathe life into a flagging group.

> *Think of it as like a shot of caffeine to a weary youth worker! (Mmm... coffee.)*

If you've got to tackle a difficult or perceived-to-be-boring topic; if they've all just had a heavy meal; if it's the end of term, then you might not be able to sail through a whole youth group session on the strength of that quick getting-to-know-you game you played at the start. An energizer is used as a secondary game – an opportunity to exercise aching muscles or reinvigorate anyone who's got a bit too comfortable on their beanbag.

> *Also, don't underplay the value of a change in pace of your activity. It's a technique that experienced teachers often use in their lessons: mixing it up. Think of these energizers as your very own adrenaline shots into the weary body of your session. (Not that your sessions are wearying or sluggish. Hopefully.)*

Indeed – a dragging youth group session might not be entirely your fault. We know that during the teenage years there's a crazy hormonal party going on inside every teenager, and that means that while sometimes they'll be bouncing off the ceiling with hyperactivity, at other times they'll be tired and drained without quite knowing why. So these games not only help you to counterbalance your own moments of dullness and low inspiration; they also work as a kind of antidote to some[5] of the effects of puberty.

92. The Praise game

Theme connection: Encouragement, community, worship

Age suitability: 11+

Resources needed: Various pens, paper, sticky tape

Venue requirements: None

Background preparation: This game involves giving the young people licence to make personal comments about one another – so there is a potential for it to be abused and go very wrong. You must not allow this to create the potential for anonymous bullying. With this in mind, choose your volunteers carefully. Also, make sure that the pens that you give to your volunteers are washable or otherwise non-marking – otherwise you could end up with lots of ruined clothes!

The game

Ask for a few volunteers, and sticky-tape a sheet of A4 paper to each of their backs. Now ask them to face one wall, and then invite the rest of the group to each take a pen and begin writing things on the backs of their volunteers. Specifically – you'd like them to write encouraging words about the person on whose back they're writing.

So challenge them to write something really nice, which they really mean, but which they might find it embarrassing to say to that person's face. Examples might include: "you're really kind"; "I really respect you"; or "I find your jokes funny". The comments can be signed or anonymous.

Give them a few minutes to think and get around all of the volunteers, then peel the bits of paper off. Quickly vet them for

---

5   To be clear, just the sluggishness. Playing these games won't stop the body odour. In fact, they may well enhance the problem.

anything inappropriate, and hand them to the person they're intended for. If this works well, you'll give your volunteers a massive shot of affirmation, and you'll get your whole group in the mood for giving praise!

What's the purpose?

Possible learning/discussion points from this game:

- Sometimes we find it difficult to say positive things to one another, or praise each other, face-to-face, but that doesn't mean we don't feel those things. This activity helps us to relax into saying nice things to our friends, which perhaps shouldn't feel as awkward as it sometimes does.

- Praise is an important part of the Christian life – one of the reasons we exist is to praise and worship the God who made us – so it's an important skill to learn!

93. Chair Stare Unaware

Theme connection: Teamwork, leadership

Age suitability: 7+

Resources needed: Enough chairs for everyone in your group

Venue requirements: Space for your chairs to be placed in a circle

Background preparation: Set your chairs out into a circle

The game

Simply get everyone sitting on chairs in a circle and pick one person to stand in the middle, remove their chair, and challenge the person in the middle to try to sit down. The rule is that the people sitting around the edge of the circle have to swap seats with someone else if they catch their eye, and as they rise and exchange seats the person in the middle has to try to sit down in one of the newly vacated seats. The beauty of this game is that not only is it a great "energizer", but it also works superbly well as an opener when kids are gradually arriving (e.g. at a lunchtime club at school…) as it can go on for as long as you like!

What's the purpose?

Possible learning/discussion points from this game:

- As a group, what was the prevailing approach to the game – were they trying to avoid catching anyone's eye, or was there a happiness to be moving about?

- Is having to do something at someone else's command something that comes naturally? Did you find yourself resenting having to move when you caught someone's eye?

94. Running Dodgeball

Theme connection: Spiritual attack, avoidance

Age suitability: 7+

Resources needed: Several foam footballs

Venue requirements: A large space

Background preparation: Mark out as large a rectangle as your space will allow, leaving enough space either side along the longer edge for a number of people to stand and move about, and enough space at either end for the whole of your group to stand without encroaching onto the rectangle.

The game

Get two volunteers or leaders to stand along the long sides with a couple of foam balls between them.

Explain to the group that in this variation of dodgeball, they have and run from the safe zone at one end of the rectangle to the other end while the people either side try to hit them below the knees with a ball. On the command everyone has to run, and anyone hit by the ball beneath the knee is out, whether it's a direct shot, a rebound, or whether it hits them while the ball continues rolling. Once they're out, they get to join one of the sides as an additional thrower trying to get the rest of the group out.

The players are only vulnerable while they run between one end and the other, but everyone has to run! Keep going until you have just a few runners left, while everyone else stands on either side trying to hit those who remain. Repeat a number of times or until you find someone who's too good and keeps winning.

What's the purpose?

Possible learning/discussion points from this game:

- What in life might you try to avoid?

- How can you protect yourself from being attacked by the works of the evil one (Ephesians 6)?

95. What's that smell?

Theme connection: Jesus, Christmas

Age suitability: 11+

Resources needed: You'll need a blindfold, and a series of clear plastic bags containing strong-smelling objects – ranging from the pleasant (ground coffee, freshly baked bread) to the positively stinky (blue cheese, damp worn socks)

Venue requirements: This game will work much better indoors

Background preparation: Prepare all the bags in advance, ideally well in advance in order to allow them to become really smelly!

The game

We can easily develop a romanticized and unrealistic image of what life was like for Jesus and his disciples – they were essentially homeless men who relied on the hospitality of others but often slept in the countryside (and even in boats). Life would have been dirty, unsanitary... and smelly. The same goes for the classic nativity scene – while it wouldn't have been in an actual barn, it would have been a pretty strong-smelling experience for Mary and Joseph!

This game helps you to get into the spirit of this rarely-talked-about reality! Select a volunteer who can take a joke (and has a strong stomach), and blindfold them. Bring out your first clear plastic bag (clear so that your watching audience can enjoy the anticipation), and open it under your volunteer's nose. Can they guess what's inside? Make the first bag a pleasant smell – e.g. fresh bread – and then follow it up with something nastier...

You could use the same volunteer throughout, or have several take it in turns. Each time they correctly identify a smell, give them a small prize. Alternatively, turn this into a competition between two volunteers – hamming up the unpleasantness of the smells to the audience.

What's the purpose?

Possible learning/discussion points from this game:

- Jesus didn't arrive on earth during the relative comfort of the modern era – God sent him into a fairly brutal, somewhat primitive culture. Jesus' life wasn't easy – in fact he made it even more unpleasant for himself by walking around the country without even a hotel budget.

- Because of things like the school nativity play or Christmas cards, we can develop a romanticized idea of what Jesus' birth and life were like. In fact they were gritty, dirty, difficult – and probably quite smelly.

96. The Number Game

Theme connection: Teamwork, achievement

Age suitability: 7+

Resources needed: None

Venue requirements: Enough space for your group to spread out across the room

Background preparation: None

The game

Instruct everyone to scatter randomly round the room and close their eyes (be careful, if you've found yourself <u>really</u> needing an energizer, make sure they don't simply fall asleep!) and then challenge them as a group to count out loud consecutively to as high a number as they can. The snag is that only one person is allowed to speak at a time, each person can only say one number at a time, and if more than one person starts to speak at the same time, then they reset and start from "one" again.

What's the purpose?

Possible learning/discussion point from this game:

* As this is quite a difficult challenge, how did they find the frustration? How did they feel about other people in the team? Did it feel like an achievement if they got to a high number?

97. Mime life story

Theme connection: Evangelism

Age suitability: 11+

Resources needed: None

Venue requirements: None

Background preparation: None

The game

Get the group to break into pairs, and explain that you're now going to tell one another your entire life story so far – without saying a word.

The first person in the pair has exactly one minute to act out the story of their entire life – from birth to the present day – in silent mime. The other person should watch closely, and at the end of the minute should attempt to tell their partner what they think that life story involved. Then switch roles, so that the other member of the pair gets to tell their story.

After the game is finished, ask the group: did anyone's mime effectively communicate their life story to their partner? If so, do they want to perform the mime again for the whole group to watch – and interpret?

What's the purpose?

Possible learning/discussion point from this game:

* It's much easier to tell a story if you use words. Christians often use this misquote of St Francis of Assisi – "preach the gospel, and if necessary use words". But the Bible seems to include lots of examples of people, including Jesus and Paul,

who preached the gospel using words – so they seem to be a pretty important part of evangelism!

98. Heads and Tails

Theme connection: Chance, prediction, the future

Age suitability: 9+

Resources needed: A coin

Venue requirements: None

Background preparation: Ensure you can flip, and catch, a coin

The game

A quick little elimination game that you can make as energetic as you like. The basic premise is that your group has to predict whether a coin you flip is going to land heads or tails. Get them to indicate their choice by running (or sedately moving, dependent on your group's energy levels) to one end of a room or the other which you have allocated as heads or tails. Once everyone's made their choice flip a coin and call out the result, eliminate all the incorrect choosers, and repeat until you have a winner.

If everyone makes the same choice, give an extra five seconds for someone to change their mind or the whole group is out. You could also adapt the means of indicating their choice to your group/setting (standing/sitting; standing on chair/standing on floor; running round/ sitting still, etc.).

What's the purpose?

Possible learning/discussion points from this game:

- What role does chance play in your life?

- Do you think you're good at predicting things?

99. Blanket Chariot Races

Theme connection: Bible, strength

Age suitability: 11+

Resources needed: Some large, thick, old blankets (it shouldn't matter if these are stretched, torn, or completely obliterated!); two objects to use as start and finish posts/lines

Venue requirements: You will need a large indoor area, ideally with a wooden floor or similar. Make sure the space is completely clear of obstacles and dangerous objects

Background preparation: None

The game

Split into two teams of equal numbers, and explain that you're going to hold a series of chariot "races". Each team should appoint two "horses" – people who are going to pull their chariot.

Now bring out the blankets, and give one to each team. Set up a start and a finish post at either end of the hall, and for the first challenge, ask the teams to choose one person to sit on their blanket and ride the "chariot" as the horses pull. They should be able to easily drag the blanket and its passenger to the finish line. If the person falls off, however, they have to go back to the start line; the "pull" only counts if the team member stays on the blanket for the whole course.

Repeat the race, but this time adding a second team member to each blanket. This time the pull will obviously be twice as hard, but it should still be possible with two people pulling. If they both achieve it, add another team member, and then another. The winning team is the one which manages to pull the highest number of people the full length of the course (without any of them falling off).

What's the purpose?

Possible learning/discussion point from this game:

- Jesus entered the world as the promised messiah – but the people expected a mighty warrior king, not a carpenter/rabbi. They were expecting the former because of their oppression by the Roman empire – which they'd hoped Jesus would overthrow. In fact, he did overthrow it – in a way – because two centuries after his death, the Roman Empire became Christian. Today Rome is the place where the Pope resides, not the seat of a mighty military empire.

100. Jump the Chicken

Theme connection: Bizarreness of life, solving problems

Age suitability: 7+

Resources needed: Several metres of rope, a rubber chicken

Venue requirements: Large open space

Background preparation: Attach the rubber chicken (or suitable alternative) securely to one end of the rope

The game

Get the young people gathered around you in a circle. They should be at a distance that measures just under what the length of rope is. Then, ensuring you have a good grip on the rope, swing the chicken (on the end of the rope) around you in a large circle a few inches above the ground. If the circle is the right distance from you the young people will need to jump over the chicken as it swings round to avoid being hit. Any time someone is hit, get them to step back out of the circle until you have one winner.

Caution: It's worth spreading the role of spinner around, as it can make you incredibly dizzy quite quickly! Also ensure that your rubber "chicken" doesn't have any hard bits on it. Or isn't a real chicken.

What's the purpose?

Possible learning/discussion point from this game:

- What (metaphorical) rubber chickens do your group find themselves needing to jump over in life?

101. Spare Chair

Theme connection: Justice, challenge

Age suitability: 9+

Resources needed: Enough chairs for everybody

Venue requirements: Enough space to set out the chairs in a circle

Background preparation: Set out the chairs in a fairly tight circle, facing inwards

The game

Get everyone apart from one person sitting down, leaving one empty seat. That "spare" person then stands in the middle, where their challenge becomes to try to sit down in an empty seat, whilst everybody else aims to ensure that they don't. The rule is this; if there is an empty seat to a person's left they must move up and sit in it before the person in the middle can sit down. If they fail to do this, they become the person in the middle.

You end up with a circle of people rotating very rapidly clockwise, and the person in the middle running around like a lunatic. This game is very simple, and can go on for ages if you are willing to let it. Chairs with arms can present bruising potential as the young people rapidly shift positions, while a scenario with chairs too far apart makes it too easy for the person in the middle. You may also need to disallow chair-hanging (akin to "goal-hanging" for fans of playground football terminology) from the person in the middle. Play for as long as you need to!

What's the purpose?

Possible learning/discussion points from this game:

- Did this game bring out a surprisingly competitive streak in anyone? Why do they think that was the case?

- How did it feel to be stuck in the middle and unable to join everyone else?

102. Dice grab

Theme connection: Justice, challenge

Age suitability: 9+

Resources needed: A pair of dice per dozen players

Venue requirements: None

Background preparation: None

The game

Get your group into a circle (of up to about a dozen max; if more than this, divide into multiple circles). Give each circle two dice and the following instructions.

The first player rolls the pair of dice, and as they do so they call out a number from two to twelve. Once the dice stop rolling, if the combined total shown matches this number, the dice become "live" and whoever can grab one scores a point for each dice they grab. If the total on the dice doesn't match the number called, simply continue on to the next person. Take it in turns to roll and call out the number, proceeding around the circle, only stopping once someone reaches a winning score of twelve points. If you can use large dice (especially foam ones) for this game, it makes it more fun!

What's the purpose?

Possible learning/discussion point from this game:

- Our resources on earth are finite – in some cases it seems that there isn't always enough to go around. What do your young people think about that?

103. Post-it cover-up

Theme connection: Identity, community, teamwork

Age suitability: 9+

Resources needed: Several pads of Post-its, pens

Venue requirements: None

Background preparation: None

The game

Divide your players into teams of about three to six, and before you do anything else get them to agree upon a team name. Once they have each done so, and you have recorded it, give each team a couple of pads of Post-it Notes and some pens.

Explain that the aim of the game is to get as many Post-it Notes as possible stuck to one of their team members within a minute. Get them to pick their team member (remembering to highlight issues of appropriateness as to where they can/can't stick their Post-its!) and explain that to prevent them from cheating, only Post-its with their team name written on them will count. Give them a second to let this sink in, and then begin the minute. At the end of the minute gently remove the stuck Post-its from the team's nominated model, and count the number of legitimately written-on Post-its to find your winning team.

What's the purpose?

Possible learning/discussion points from this game:

- Does your identity come from external or internal sources?

- Does sharing a task with your teammates make you feel more or less like a team?

104. Silent Lines

Theme connection: Communication, identity
Age suitability: 9+
Resources needed: None
Venue requirements: None
Background preparation: None

The game

Firstly, instruct your group to line themselves up, without help, in order of height. Once they have mastered this (hopefully) simple instruction, introduce a new element – that they have to fulfil their next task without speaking. This time get them to sort themselves in order of age. Then make it more difficult by getting them to order themselves by date of birth but excluding year – so you have 1 January at one extreme, right down to 31 December at the other.

If you feel so inspired you can obviously get them to order themselves using any other suitable criteria, or blindfold them. This activity can also be used for dividing your group into teams without the usual faffing about – once they're in line simply count them off into the number of teams you need.

What's the purpose?

Possible learning/discussion points from this game:

- Do you ever worry about where you fit in?

- Do you find it easier to communicate without words?

105. True or False?

Theme connection: Truth, lies, discernment

Age suitability: 11+

Resources needed: A "true" sign and a "false" sign, small chocolate prize

Venue requirements: This can theoretically work anywhere, but might work best in a larger space with two distinct "ends" for people to run between

Background preparation: Have a good look at www.snopes.com to find some brilliant examples of urban legend. Hang the "true" and "false" signs at opposite ends of your venue

The game

Explain that you're going to read a series of statements which sound surprising or ridiculous... but only some of them aren't true. They have to try to sort fact from fiction – and they do that by running to the appropriate end of the room to signify whether they think each statement is true or false. Reveal the correct answer after all the young people have picked an end – all those who got the answer wrong sit out, and you play again with the remainder. See if you can whittle down your group to a single winner – and award them a small prize.

The statements:

- The modern image of Santa Claus was created by Coca-Cola (false).
- Photographic images of a naked lady are hidden in the Disney film "The Rescuers" (true).
- Finland once banned Donald Duck because he wears no pants (false).
- By proclamation of Governor George W. Bush, 10 June 2000 was "Jesus Day" in Texas (true).
- Sirloin steak is so named because an English king enjoyed it so much, he knighted it, making it "Sir Loin" (false).
- The orchestral theme from the TV show Star Trek has secret lyrics (true).
- Walt Disney's body has been cryogenically frozen – and he could be brought back to life if defrosted (false).

You could of course add your own statements, tailored toward your group

What's the purpose?

Possible learning/discussion point from this game:

- Sometimes it's hard to tell truth from fiction. What we need is discernment (Hebrews 5:14 offers a great explanation of this) to be able to tell the difference – and that's something that we can ask God for.

7

Messy Games

Baked beans are my kryptonite.

It was the New Malden Baptist Church summer fete, circa 1995. They were looking for volunteers for a food-based game, and as a chubby extrovert, I was up the front faster than you could say "Krispy Kreme". But as I donned the blindfold, little did I know that I was just moments away from being forced to consume a spoonful of cold Heinz 57. It was a nightmare, and I suffer regular flashbacks even to this day.

Of course, as a seasoned youth worker, I now know that the use of baked beans in a blindfolded food game was almost inevitable. That's because they're both cheap and gloriously messy – two key ingredients of any great youth ministry prop. Young people just love a messy game.

> I tell you who doesn't though:
>
> ...
>
> Yup, that's right. Nobody. Well, except maybe parents when their little darlings get covered in shaving foam and food dye. Or perhaps the committee which is in charge of the church hall where you meet, who don't like the splatters of mashed banana that now adorn the ceiling. But that's probably it. The young people love it, though, and as long as you prepare appropriately, so will you and your team!
>
> (On a side-note, though, Martin – if baked beans are your kryptonite, what was your Fortress of Solitude?)

(Good question, Jimmy. As a porky and unpopular teenager, it was definitely McDonald's. But let me tell you something, friend: they might call it a Happy Meal, but it only makes you sadder.)

Anyway, in short: messy games are fantastic fun. Don't focus on all the cleaning up you'll have to do afterwards (really clever youth workers just make that part of the activity anyway, though we should mention here that a tarpaulin or plastic sheet is an essential part of the kit for the activities that follow); see it as a great opportunity to get young people laughing, mixing, and interacting. You can pretty much guarantee it'll be the thing they're telling their friends about at school the next morning. Just, please, be mindful of the baked bean haters of the world when you're shopping for that blindfolded taste-test. We're a small but vocal minority.

106. Banana split race

Theme connection: Faith, the future

Age suitability: 11+

Resources needed: Small bananas (unpeeled), several cans of squirty cream, glacé cherries, chocolate sprinkles, paper bibs, towels for clean-up

Venue requirements: Make sure you hold this activity in a venue where it doesn't matter if you spill cream or squash bananas on the floor!

Background preparation: As with any game involving food, make sure you assess risks in advance. Are there any allergies in your group? Does anyone have issues with food? Is there a qualified first-aider on hand if something goes wrong?

The game

Split your group into several teams (between two and four, depending on how many ingredients you have), and invite each team to nominate a "champion" to take part in an eating competition. Once you have your volunteers, give them paper bibs (paper towels will do), and line them up on a surface where it's easy to mop up spills (so not carpet!). As they're lining up, explain that this game is called a "banana split race".

Now reveal the twist – your volunteers will be making the banana splits… in their stomachs! They'll be fed the component ingredients –

bananas, squirty cream, glacé cherries, and chocolate sprinkles – and it's a race to be the first to eat them all before their opponents.

Now choose a responsible volunteer or leader to represent each team as "feeder". This person's role is to feed the ingredients to the "eater", and to do so in such a way that ensures the person doesn't choke (!). Be careful to stress this to all your contestants.

Encourage each team to get behind their contestants with plenty of cheering and enthusiasm. Award a prize – perhaps a bunch of bananas – to the victorious team, and provide towels to clean everyone up.

What's the purpose?

Possible learning/discussion point from this game:

- Use this game as an illustration that sometimes we don't see what God is planning – sometimes we only get glimpses of the end result. Indeed, sometimes we will never see what God was doing in and through our lives until we're looking back at them with him in eternity.

107. The Hanging Doughnut game

Theme connection: Consumption, greed

Age suitability: 9+

Resources needed: A supply of ring doughnuts (the mini ones, available from most large supermarkets, are best, bearing in mind factors like budget/time/comedy-value/potential for mess), a supply of elastic (or if not available, some wool or any kind of string; the bounce of elastic just makes it more difficult for the competitors), and something to hang the doughnuts from. A clothes horse (upright clothes drier) balanced securely between two chairs or tables works well, or failing that any kind of rope/bar that can be suspended above the ground

Venue requirements: A floor that can cope with crumbs of doughnut falling all over it (i.e. not carpeted)

Background preparation: Tie each doughnut to a piece of elastic and then attach that to your drier/pole/whatever you decide to use so that the doughnuts are hanging above the ground at a low height (anything between 30 and 80 cm provides maximum "enjoyment")

The game

This game is a relay race, so divide your group into teams and send them to one end of your hall/room. At the opposite end, suspend the appropriate number of doughnuts for each team member to have at least one, and instruct the young people that it's a race to be the first team to consume all the doughnuts without using their hands. Explain that in the manner of a classic relay race, one person at a time runs up to the front, eats a (single) doughnut, and must return to their team before the next person can have their turn. Inform them that if any chunks of doughnut fall to the floor, you will impose a time-penalty of five seconds for each piece as you deem appropriate (this is probably a better idea than getting your young people to eat off the floor, no matter how clean the floor in your venue… or how much your group try to persuade you the five-second rule is a valid scientific fact. It's not, I Googled it).

Once everyone has had a go and their doughnuts are all consumed, get the team to show they've finished by holding their stomachs and groaning loudly "I feel sick". (Or they might do that naturally, depending on how many doughnuts they've had to consume.) As with any games involving food, be sensitive to any young people who may have issues with this.

What's the purpose?

Possible learning/discussion points from this game:

- Are we greedy as a society?
- Can your group connect to the issue of spending a lot of time and effort to get something that turns out not to be worth a great deal?

108. Stick your nose in

Theme connection: Sin, carrying burdens

Age suitability: 9+

Resources needed: A large bag of Maltesers, a jar of chocolate spread, several bowls

Venue requirements: A floor that won't suffer from chocolate spread smears or crushed Maltesers. (Not carpeted)

Background preparation: Set out two empty bowls at one end of your room, and two bowls full of Maltesers at the other end. Make sure there are no nut allergies amongst your group before using chocolate spread! Jam/Marmite or similar should work as an alternative if needed

The game

The challenge of the game is to move a bowlful of Maltesers, using only a nose smeared in chocolate spread, from one place to another, in this case from one end of the room to the other. This game works best as a relay race, so divide your group into two teams and give each team one of the bowls full of "lightly honeycombed rounded chocolates" and one of the empty "target" bowls placed at the other end of the room.

Place a dollop of chocolate spread on the nose of each participant and explain that one at a time they need to pick up as many Maltesers as they can (using only their nose) and to carry them (again, only using their nose) to the bowl at the other end of the hall. Once they have successfully deposited their cargo they return to their team and the next person has a go.

Any dropped Maltesers are returned to the first bowl and the winning team is the first to transport all their Maltesers to the second bowl. Tips: allow carrying of multiple Maltesers as it's nigh on impossible to pick up only one at a time! Be warned, this game has potential for smeary chocolate mess. Not a great game for carpeted areas or white T-shirts.

Needless to say, if you are feeling generous and want to give prizes for any of these games, the prize should be some form of chocolate. Or perhaps a toothbrush!

What's the purpose?

Possible learning/discussion points from this game:

- Jesus said "Come to me all who are weary and burdened" (Matthew 11:28). Do your group ever feel like they are weary or burdened?

- Sin is messy, and it sticks to us – in fact we just can't get it off on our own.

109. After-Eight Face

Theme connection: Self-control, perseverance, persistence

Age suitability: 9+

Resources needed: A box of After-Eights (or similar thin chocolate-covered mints)

Venue requirements: None

Background preparation: None

The game

Take a box of After-Eights (or an alternative non-branded, thin, square after-dinner mint covered in chocolate!) and a load of young people with heads tilting back. Balance the mints (out of their wrappers!) onto the forehead of each participant. The challenge is then to get the mint into the mouth without using hands or anything else other than the face. It sounds easy, yet is surprisingly difficult and funny to watch.

This can be an up-front game, a team race, or an everybody-together-at-the-same-time thing. Tip: have something to hand to wipe any faces free of melted chocolate trails!

What's the purpose?

Possible learning/discussion points from this game:

- Do you view persistence as a positive quality or potentially negative?

- Sometimes difficult and painful situations can have positive pay-offs. Can your group think of examples from their own lives? What about from the Bible?

110. Wotsits? What's that?

Theme connection: Sin, putting burdens onto others

Age suitability: 9+

Resources needed: Shaving foam, light corn-based crisps (e.g. Wotsits), bowl of water, towel

Venue requirements: An easily cleanable surface for playing on (not carpet!) or a removable covering like a tarpaulin

Background preparation: None

The game

Divide your group into equal teams, and get each team to find a member willing to be a target. Take that person and carefully cover their face with shaving foam (make sure to leave a gap around the nose for breathing, and avoiding the eyes as the soapy foam can sting!) and give the other team members a packet of Wotsits each (or other cheaper, generic equivalent). Get the foam-faced target people to stand or sit a short distance away from a line in front of their team (distance as appropriate for the age/size of your group – about two metres should be suitable).

Position the rest of their teams behind the line and explain that their job is to take it in turns to throw the Wotsits at their teammate to try to get the crisps to stick to their face. The winning team will be the team with the most Wotsits stuck to the shaving foam (still on the person's face) at the end. You don't need to set a time limit, just ensure that each team has the same number of packets of Wotsits to throw (one bag per team member is ideal, budget allowing). Just ensure that any Wotsits that are thrown and don't stick aren't re-thrown.

Once each team has thrown all the Wotsits, get a leader to remove any that have stuck to the shaving foam and count them up. Provide a bowl of water and towel for washing the foam off the face. Reward the winning team with a non-shaving-foam-coated packet of Wotsits.

What's the purpose?

Possible learning/discussion points from this game:

- What sort of things do you find "stick" in your life?

- What habits/behaviours are hard to give up/get rid of?

- There's a famous saying that "a problem shared is a problem halved". Do you find this to be true, or do you simply find that you're transferring your problem onto someone else?

111. Doughnut trials

Theme connection: Character, temptation

Age suitability: 11+

Resources needed: Jam doughnuts. Be careful in selecting these – the great variety of doughnuts now available makes this tricky. You're looking for jam-filled doughnuts covered in sugar granules, not a dusting of icing sugar. You can usually get these at a bakery; supermarket versions tend not to work quite so well

Venue requirements: This game can get a little bit messy, so make sure you're somewhere that you can spill jam

Background preparation: Ensure you are aware of any food allergies or issues in your group

The game

This game is split into two parts (although obviously you don't have to do both of them). The first is a race; the second is a test in self-control.

Choose a few volunteers to take part in the race, and hand out a sugary jam doughnut to each of them. Explain that on your command, they'll begin a race to see who can remove every granule of sugar from their doughnut first. If one of them claims to have done it, shout "freeze", and inspect their doughnut (get them to hold it!). If you see any sugar at all, restart the race; otherwise, congratulate the winner. They can eat their doughnuts now!

Choose another batch of volunteers for the second challenge. This time it's not a race but a test – to see who can eat an entire doughnut without licking either their fingers or, most importantly, their lips. Have leaders or other volunteers watching each competitor carefully for signs of a flicking tongue. This challenge is much harder than it sounds!

What's the purpose?

Possible learning/discussion point from this game:

- The Christian life is all about developing character, to become more like Jesus. When he was walking around on earth, Jesus showed great strength of character in the way he interacted with others – and as we seek to be like him, we should try to learn perseverance, resistance to temptation, and self-control.

112. Saturated rounders

Theme connection: Water of life, refreshment

Age suitability: 9+

Resources needed: Foam ball, bucket of water, four "bases"

Venue requirements: This game needs to take place outside

Background preparation: Set out the bases in a baseball-style diamond, and soak the foam ball in the bucket of water

The game

You and your group are probably familiar with the game of baseball/ rounders (dependent on local variations) and you probably have your own variation of rules, but here's a new, wetter, extra-fun version of that game.

In this variant, substitute a foam football soaked in a bucket of water for the ball, and make the young people kick it rather than using a bat. To get people out, simply hit them with the ball as they try to make their way round the bases. Keep a bucket by the pitcher's spot, and "refresh" the ball in between players.

What's the purpose?

Possible learning/discussion points from this game:

- Jesus is the water of life. Discuss.

- On a hot day this can be a very refreshing game – what refreshes your group?

113. Water shifter

Theme connection: Creation, justice, teamwork

Age suitability: 11+

Resources needed: One bucket (or other water containers) per team, plus one larger water receptacle, assorted craft resources (paper, cling film wrap, plastic cup, funnel, toilet rolls, etc.)

Venue requirements: Outside

Background preparation: Fill a large bucket of water

The game

Divide your group into small teams (about three to six people, depending on abundance of resources) and give each team an equal pile of stuff that they have to use to construct a mechanism to move water from the large water receptacle at one end of your playing arena to their particular bucket (one per team) at the other end of the space.

Use your creativity (or whatever you have lying around!) to provide these resources. Give them a time limit within which they must construct their carrier, and also get as much water shifted as possible. Introduce a rule that each member of the team must carry their receptacle at least part of the way between the buckets, and also that they are not allowed to directly hold the thing that is holding the water (e.g. if you give them a plastic cup they aren't allowed to simply carry the plastic cup full of water – they could hold something that is supporting the cup, but no direct contact is allowed!).

At the end of the time limit (fifteen minutes is probably enough – but this depends on the group) see which team's bucket has the most water. Declare them the winners. (Perhaps give them a bottle of water as a prize.)

What's the purpose?

Possible learning/discussion points from this game:

- There are communities in parts of the world which do not have safe supplies of drinking water. What does this say about us?

- How would you feel if you had to manually transport every drop of water you used? Would it affect the way you used it?

114. Run the Gauntlet

Theme connection: Challenge, overcoming difficulties

Age suitability: 9+

Resources needed: Cans of shaving foam, various water pistols

Venue requirements: Play outside, preferably in a large open space

Background preparation: Mark out your playing area, with a "safe zone" at each end

The game

Divide your group into two teams, and, using the shaving foam, draw big crosses on the backs of each member of <u>one</u> of those teams. Take them to one end of your playing area and explain that they have to try to get to the other side and safety while retaining as much of the cross as possible. Equip the other team with sprayers/water pistols, etc. and instruct them to dot themselves across the "arena" and try to wash off as much of the crosses as possible once the other team start to run, and before they get to a safe area. Count down three, two, one… and let the mayhem commence. Swap the roles over and repeat.

What's the purpose?

Possible learning/discussion points from this game:

- Does the idea of a difficult task like this fill your group with dread or excitement? Why?

- How much of life feels like this for your group?

115. Duck, Duck, Splash

Theme connection: Being chosen
Age suitability: 9+
Resources needed: A bucket of water, source of water to refill it
Venue requirements: This game should be played outside
Background preparation: Fill your bucket with water

The game

A game based on the old standard "duck, duck, goose". Get the young people seated in a circle with one person walking round the outside of the circle, splashing water from a bucket/bowl onto the heads of the participants one at a time (i.e. duck). At some random stage they then dump the entire contents of the bucket onto the next poor unsuspecting victim (goose) who then has to rise from their seat and attempt to tag the soaker, who needs to try to run around the circle and back into the empty spot where the newly wet person had been sitting before they are tagged.

If they manage to get there without being tagged, they get to sit down, and the "goose" becomes the new soaker. If they are tagged, however, the goose gets their seat back, and the soaker continues in their role.

Tip: it might be worth your while swapping the prize for catching the "soaker" – as your group may consider being the "soaker" to be the better prize. In which case switch it so that if the goose tags the soaker then they get to be the new soaker.

What's the purpose?

Possible learning/discussion point from this game:

- Is being chosen (or singled out) generally a good thing or not in your young people's experience?

8

Tech Games

I will always be indebted to my father for the introduction he gave me to the technological world. As a computer engineer in the 1980s, he would regularly bring home bits of tech which he'd either "borrowed" from work "for testing", or early-adopted from the local computing shop. He'd programme our ZX81 for hours so that I could guide a little man around a simple maze; we'd barely be able to contain our excitement as a game of "Horace Goes Skiing" loaded (over the course of three long minutes) on the tape deck of our Sinclair Spectrum 48k. Most memorably, we once made a talking computer, with a vocabulary of fifty words, say the phrase "I have gone for a we(e) we(e)", over and over again. I'm pretty sure I owe my comfort with the brave new digital world to the platform he created.

> *Wow, it's like the Bill Gates story all over again. I grew up with a BBC micro computer – and my formative gaming experience was shaped by a game called Chuckie Egg, which was a platform game where you ran round a world populated by giant walking birds collecting what was (presumably) their eggs and seeds. In many ways it was a natural leap from that to Angry Birds, albeit with the player on a different side (I hunted it down on the internet recently, and it was just as good as I remembered it. I like to think that I was part of the zeitgeist that led to the Angry Birds franchise)...*

What was true for me then is still true for young people now – teenagers love technology. They're comfortable with it, they're largely fascinated by it, and they understand its potential to change the world even better than most of the rest of us do. Mainly though, they love it because of the potential it offers to play games.

I sometimes wonder whether my trepidation of approaching nesting birds owes more to my membership of The Young Ornithologists' Club as a young and enthusiastic nature lover, or to a misplaced sense of guilt about those poor birds whose eggs I stole in Chuckie Egg.

Now, this section won't offer you a gaming experience to rival Call of Duty, but it's still packed full of fun (and hopefully a lot less brutal killing).

116. What is it?

Theme connection: Seeing clearly

Age suitability: 7+

Resources needed: Laptop with presentation software, e.g. PowerPoint; projector (or with smaller groups, you may just use the laptop screen), small chocolate prizes

Venue requirements: You'll need an indoor space in which it's possible to project onto a screen or wall – unless you're in a smaller group

Background preparation: Before your meeting, take some close-up or strangely composed photographs of your meeting room. You need to find a balance between making them obscure, and eventually guessable. Subjects might include: a carpet stain; a close-up shot of a mug; part of a poster or display that's hanging on your venue wall. Now take these photos and put them into a PowerPoint or Keynote presentation

The game

Settle your group and ask everyone to look at the screen. Flash up the first image – can anyone guess what it is? Don't reveal at first that this image is actually part of your meeting room. Now show the rest of the images – can anyone guess what these are? Hopefully no one will guess correctly!

Now restart the presentation, but this time explain the secret: these photos were all taken inside this room. Allow people to move around the room if they want to – and give them a good amount of time to guess each one before you move on to the next slide.

Award prizes to anyone who guesses correctly, and give hints as necessary on the more difficult ones.

What's the purpose?

Possible learning/discussion point from this game:

* The Bible says we see "through a glass darkly" (1 Corinthians 13:12) – the full revelation of God's person and power only comes when we're in eternity. This game simulates that glass quite well!

117. Backwards Karaoke

Theme connection: Truth, perspective

Age suitability: 11+

Resources needed: Ability to record and reverse audio (a computer with simple – i.e. free – audio-editing software such as Audacity[6] should be able to do this), speakers

Venue requirements: None

Background preparation: Print out some short sections of lyrics from famous songs

---

6   Audacity is a freely downloadable audio clipping programme, available from www.audacity.sourceforge.net. Other similar programmes are available, but this one is simple and easy to use.

The game

Divide your group into small groups of two or three and give each of them some lyrics to attempt to recite backwards. Record each group doing so on a computer, then reverse the recordings and play back to see which group got closest to clearly communicating their message. Once they've heard how far off they are (or not), let them record the message forwards and then reverse that so they can have a go at imitating it. Record again and reverse as before.

What's the purpose?

Possible learning/discussion points from this game:

- What seems back to front in life?

- If God's kingdom is back to front compared to the way the world sees things (the last shall be first, turn the other cheek, the greatest shall serve the least, etc.), what does this have to say about the way we should live our lives?

118. Photo Treasure Hunt

Theme connection: Discovery, value

Age suitability: 11+

Resources needed: Camera phones, laptop, lists of items for each team. If your group won't have access to camera phones, you can still find packs of disposable one-use cameras which you can give out and collect for developing at the end (but you would need to run the end of the game differently, perhaps splitting it over two sessions.

Venue requirements: None

Background preparation: Write a list of objects/scenarios that you want your groups to photograph

The game

Break up your group into threes or fours, and ensure that each group has access to a camera (utilizing the ubiquitous camera phones). Give each group a list of items/poses/scenes to photograph and send them off around the building/area to take photos of as many of them as they can within the time frame – a list of twenty scenarios should be an achievable challenge within forty-five minutes.

Make the list as creative and fun as possible, mixing up difficult to find/unusual/gross objects with silly poses and some artistic challenges (e.g. something that looks like a member of your group, something ordinary in an extraordinary place, dog poo, an unusual perspective, something spiritual, etc.). Let the group know that you will be marking them on artistic ability, creative interpretation of instructions (e.g. when doing this recently one group made a scarily realistic dog and dog poo using Lego – bonus points!), and of course points for a completed list.

Make sure your group understand the time limits and boundaries of where they are allowed to go (ensuring this is safe and suitable for your group) and send them off.

When they return you will want to collect the photos onto a central computer so you can show them off easily, so make sure that you can transfer them – if you can, get them to Bluetooth the pictures directly from their phones to a laptop (work out in advance how to do this!) or failing that perhaps get them to Bluetooth them to your phone and you can upload them to your computer at your leisure.

If you can do it quickly put some of the (edited!) highlights up on the screen or projector for the group to enjoy straight away, or alternatively take them away and create a slideshow using the pictures ready to start your next session or Sunday's service with!

What's the purpose?

Possible learning/discussion points from this game:

- What do you value the most?

- How far would you go to find something you "treasure"?

119. Know your Net

Theme connection: Online behaviour, online safety

Age suitability: 11+

Resources needed: Computer, projector, small chocolate prizes

Venue requirements: You'll need an indoor space in which it's possible to project onto a screen or wall – unless you're in a smaller group, in which case you can use the laptop screen

Background preparation: Create your own short (five-slide) website recognition game, where each slide reveals a very small, zoomed-in or obscure part of a famous website. Ideas might include the "like" button on Facebook, the "Breaking News" ticker on the BBC News website, or the comments section of a YouTube video page.

The game

Before showing the slides, ask: what are your favourite websites? What kinds of things do you tend to use the internet for? Which sites do you visit every single day? What about less often?

Now show the slides, one by one, and see if anyone can work out which websites or platforms they represent. Award a small prize to the first person to correctly guess each one. As you reveal the correct answer, take a few moments to find out how the group feels about this particular website.

What's the purpose?

Possible learning/discussion points from this game:

- This simple recognition game will introduce the subject of internet use, and help to tease out some of the ways that the group members are already comfortable with sharing and interacting online.

- We all use the internet, every day. Just as in real life, we can make positive or negative decisions about how we behave and interact with others online. We can also easily hide our online behaviour from others (e.g. looking at internet porn). Obviously, the topics you discuss will vary depending on the age group.

120. The Intro Game

Theme connection: Identity

Age suitability: 11+

Resources needed: Speakers, a computer, pens, paper

Venue requirements: An indoor space that is relatively quiet

Background preparation: Record short snippets of popular/ famous songs, which you play back to your group and they then need to identify the song title and artist from that short clip. About ten clips is an ideal number, and the best thing is to provide a mix of "classic" pop songs – think The Beatles/Kylie/Rage Against the Machine (delete as appropriate) – alongside the stuff that's in the charts currently.

A good and easy way of finding popular current music is to use Spotify (free version available), or perhaps the previews from the iTunes store. Record short sections of these using Audacity (or another recording programme on your computer) and then save to some form of music player from which you can play the clips to your youth group via loudspeakers. Ensure you don't accidentally include the title of the song and/or chorus in the snippets, and definitely make sure you remember which clip is which so that you know the correct answers when it comes to marking!

The game

Give your group a piece of paper and pen each, and get them to write down the band/artist and song title for each clip you play. Play each clip twice, don't allow any conferring, and then find out which member of your group knows the most about music!

Bonus feature: this game is also a wonderful opportunity to "educate" your group as to the kind of music that you think they should be listening to, aka the kind of stuff that was in the "hit-parade" when you were out "grooving" in "discotheques".

What's the purpose?

Possible learning/discussion points from this game:

- What kind of music are your group into? Why?

- How do their tastes differ from those of their parents?

- Do they think that there are some songs that it isn't appropriate to listen to? Why might that be?

121. Missing slide

Theme connection: Memory, concentration

Age suitability: 11+

Resources needed: Computer, projector, small chocolate prizes

Venue requirements: You'll need an indoor space in which it's possible to project onto a screen or wall – unless you're in a smaller group, in which case you can use the laptop screen

Background preparation: Prepare a PowerPoint (or similar) presentation containing ten to twelve images of objects, people, famous places, album covers, stills from popular TV shows, etc., then the same set of images in a different order with one removed. (You may want to prepare a second presentation with different images in case this proves popular!)

The game

This is a hi-tech version of the classic "objects on a tray" game.

Challenge the whole group to memorize the sequence you're about to play. Play the slides through slowly to the group, perhaps stopping to comment briefly on each. Depending on how well (or otherwise) you think they were concentrating, you might choose to play that first complete sequence through again.

Now explain that you're going to play the same images again in a different order, but with one image removed – can they work out which one is missing?

Play the second sequence, and award a small prize to the first person who tells you which image was missing. If you want to make the game easier, put the second run of images in the same order as the first, but again with one image removed (it's easier to remember a break in a familiar sequence).

From experience, this game can be quite popular and over quite quickly, so you may wish to prepare a second sequence of images in order to play another round.

What's the purpose?

Possible learning/discussion points from this game:

- Concentration is a virtue – it helps us to get into the Bible; it helps us with schoolwork and exams.

- It's important that we hold on to our memories of God and our faith journey. When we face doubts, these memories become vital in reminding us of the reason for our hope in Jesus.

122. Audio Traffic Lights

Theme connection: Obedience, instinct

Age suitability: 7+

Resources needed: MP3 player/computer, speakers

Venue requirements: Large hall

Background preparation: Record a series of individual and distinct sounds, as many as you need to correspond to instructions

The game

Traffic lights is a simple game where single-word commands instruct players to move to particular areas of your playing space, or to do certain actions. In a basic form, the four walls of the room are labelled as appropriate "North", "South", "East", and "West", and on the instruction to "drop" all the players have to sit down. The beauty of this game is that you can use any instructions (e.g. local geography, or make up your own silly actions – let your imagination run wild!) and then you simply knock out the last person in the group to recognize and complete each instruction until you have a winner.

Run this game the traditional way, and then reveal that you're going to attempt an advanced version. Explain that instead of verbal instructions you're going to play sounds, each of which will represent a particular instruction. In preparation you'll need as many individual and distinct sounds as you want to have instructions, and a means of playing them loudly so that all the players can hear them (an MP3 player linked to speakers will work adequately); the more comical the sounds the better. Clearly explain which sound goes with which response/section of the room, and let the fun begin. After a couple of trial rounds, begin knocking out the slowest responder of each round.

What's the purpose?

Possible learning/discussion points from this game:

- Do your group find it hard to overcome instincts and learn new instructions?

- Do your group find themselves doing certain things in certain situations? Why do we do this?

123. Distorted faces

Theme connection: Celebrity, seeing clearly

Age suitability: 8+

Resources needed: Laptop and projector, flipchart or other scoreboard, optional chocolate prize

Venue requirements: You'll need an indoor space in which it's possible to project onto a screen or wall

Background preparation: Ahead of the meeting, create some images of famous celebrities which have been digitally distorted to hide their identity (this website will enable you to do this easily: http://william.hoza.us/warp/). Distort them so they're hard, but not impossible, to recognize. The website above will give you a few examples, but you may also want to upload some images of other famous people, and even members of your leadership team, to personalize the game.

The game

Split the group into two teams. Project the first face onto the screen, and explain that this is a famous person. Invite the first team to guess at who it might be – they only get one guess per team. If they get it right, award them a point; if they get it wrong, give the other team a go. Even if they then score a point, it's their turn next.

Alternate between the teams, and award a small prize to the team with the most correct guesses.

What's the purpose?

Possible learning/discussion points from this game:

- We know our famous celebrities so well that we can recognize many of them even when their image has been distorted – so do we know them too well?

- Sometimes we can find it difficult to understand or hear from God. We long to hear him clearly, but often we feel like we're not getting the full picture. By concentrating on his voice, and with the help of others, we can begin to understand him more clearly.

124. Google Map Game

Theme connection: Wider world, culture

Age suitability: 9+

Resources needed: Maps for each team

Venue requirements: Enough space to spread maps out on the floor

Background preparation: Prepare your list of places for your teams to find, and ensure that you know where to find them on the maps

The game

Divide your group into teams and give each team a map. The teams can be anything between two and five (basically as many as you can realistically fit around a map spread out on the floor) and the maps all need to be of a decent size and the same.

There are two ways you could play this game – for the first method, the map needs to be a generic one of the particular part of the world (or country) that you have chosen. In this set-up, you give the teams a list of say fifteen particular places which they need to try and mark onto the map, and you award points based on how accurate you judge them to be: ten points for spot-on, and then decreasing amounts depending on how far away they are or how generous you're feeling. The team with the highest score at the end of your list is the winning team.

In the second method, the map you give them is a more detailed map, with place names and so on already marked on it (at whatever scale you want – it works with world, national, or local level). Pick about ten places on the map for them to find, and then give the places to the teams one at a time, revealing the next place to find only once they've found the previous location on the map. The winning team is therefore the first one to find all the locations that you require.

To make this game more funny/juvenile/better (delete as applicable) you could deliberately ensure that all the place names they need to find sound vaguely rude. (Someone's already done the work for you at http://maps.geotastic.org/vaguely-rude-places/index.html)

What's the purpose?

Possible learning/discussion points from this game:

- Do you feel like a citizen of the world?

- How far would you go to share good news? How far would you expect others to come to you to share good news?

125. Name that anthem

Theme connection: Wider world, culture, identity

Age suitability: 9+

Resources needed: MP3 player, speakers

Venue requirements: None

Background preparation: Download a dozen clips of different national anthems, picking a variety of obscure and obvious countries

The game

Play the clips one at a time to your group – getting them to write down which nation's anthem they think it is. Give them a list of the possible countries to aid them, or (to make it more difficult) do so in the form of the flags. Alternatively, don't provide a list of countries and rely on their geographical knowledge.

What's the purpose?

Possible learning/discussion points from this game:

- Where in the world have you been/do you want to go?

- What difference (if any) does your nationality make to your identity?

126. Meme me

Theme connection: Technology, social media, identity

Age suitability: 11+

Resources needed: A camera per team, a computer to share pictures on

Venue requirements: None

Background preparation: None

The game

Divide your group into teams, make sure that each one of them has access to a camera, and set them the task of replicating a famous internet meme by being as creative as possible. Give them a set of suggestions and pictures of cats/double rainbows/cute animals/planking/ice bucket challenges and see how creative they can be at replicating them.

Make sure that their ideas are safe (!) and then get the groups to share with each other what meme they were aiming to replicate, and the picture they took of themselves. If you want to you, could ask the groups to vote for which is the best replication, or you could simply agree that they are all winners just for doing something so pointless and silly.

What's the purpose?

Possible learning/discussion points from this game:

- What do they think will last in popular culture?

- Why do they think particular memes take root in our collective imaginations? What does this say about us as individuals?

127. i-message-u

Theme connection: Technology, communication

Age suitability: 9+

Resources needed: A set of the following for **each** team: a long stretch of string, two cups (or tins), something to make holes in the bottom of the cups/tins, two flags, and a bright torch, plus two printouts of each of the following: the Semaphore alphabet, the Morse code alphabet, and the British Sign Language alphabet; paper, pens

Venue requirements: A large hall or long corridors to play in

Background preparation: Print out the copies of the three alphabets, and a message for the teams to pass along the chain

The game

Divide your groups into teams of five and give each team a pile of equipment which includes: a long stretch of string, two cups (or tins), two flags, and a bright torch, plus two printouts of each of the following: the Semaphore alphabet, the Morse code alphabet, and the British Sign Language alphabet.

Explain that they need to use four different means of quiet or silent communication to pass a message from one end of the team to another. Allow them to work out how they will do it, and what set-up they want to employ (provide a bit of help with the strings/cup telephone idea if they aren't getting it). Explain that once they've got the whole team stretched out with the varying means of communication between them, you will give a short message (comprising a simple sentence, such as, "West Ham United are the greatest") to the first team member who then needs to communicate it to the next, and so on, until it reaches the final team member, who then needs to confirm to you what message they've received.

If the message isn't right get them to try again, until you have a correct answer. This will work best if you have a large space or long corridors to play it in, or it can also work outside if conditions are right. You will also need to give each team paper and pens so they can note down the letters as they are spelled, but ensure they don't cheat by using the paper to communicate with each other!

What's the purpose?

Possible learning/discussion points from this game:

- Does the increased variety of communications/social media make it easier or more difficult to properly convey a message?

- Do we rely on technology too much?

9

Team Games

Teamwork is an essential life skill. No one ever wrote on their CV that they "struggle to work well with others", and if they did, they're probably either unemployed or working in a railway signal box.

> *Can I just highlight how terrifying the idea is of a whole bunch of individuals, who don't want to be part of a team, all working independently in railway signal boxes across the country, refusing to work with each other... I really hope that's not the case.*

For most of us though, working as part of a team to achieve things is an important part of everyday life, whether that's in the context of work, home, or church. Companies with a strong sense of team are good at pulling together to overcome challenges; families where the members work with instead of turning against one another have a better sense of thriving. It's true in sport too: in Spanish football the two top teams of recent years are often characterized as opposites in this regard. Barcelona are a team who work hard for one another; Real Madrid are a collection of highly feted and hugely expensive superstars who appear to be competing with one another to be the greatest. No prizes for guessing which of those teams has been more successful.

> *Typical comment of a West Ham fan. (Joking – as an Arsenal fan I'm just bitter about Barcelona always poaching our players and then knocking us out of the Champions League.)*

So when we play team games in our youth group, we're not only having fun (and perhaps introducing a teaching point);

(cough – definitely having a purpose to the game)

we're also investing in the skill of teamwork. And in a culture of individualism, that's not insignificant.

And on a more practical note, games which involve everyone are often a much better idea than games which only involve a couple of people. And let's face it, the illustration of church as a body that works together is hardly an original one (copyright © Paul, 1st C. AD) – games are a wonderful way of helping your young people begin to understand that connection.

128. Newspaper agenda scavenger hunt

Theme connection: Culture, media, politics

Age suitability: 14+

Resources needed: Whiteboard or flipchart and pen, small chocolate prizes, lots of different newspapers, vetted for inappropriate content (!)

Venue requirements: None

Background preparation: If possible, find editions of newspapers which have some stories with church or faith-based content, such as quotes from the Archbishop of Canterbury or another leading church figure

The game

Make lots of recent newspapers available – ideally enough so that there's one per person. Split the young people into groups of four to five, and distribute the newspapers.

Explain you're going to be conducting a kind of "scavenger hunt" – and they need to find as many of the following list as possible within their newspapers. Display this list on a whiteboard, flipchart, or similar:

Can you find:

- An advert for a charity? (Extra point for a weird one!)
- A photo of an insect
- A story with a quote from a Christian
- A pun (or other joke) headline
- An article about an obscure sport
- A story about religion
- A positive or good news story
- A mention of atheism, secularism, or a famous atheist
- A review of something
- A picture of something which doesn't exist in real life

Once they've found something, they should rip out the relevant page and give it to their nominated group leader. The only rule is that they can't use the same page for two categories. At the end of five minutes, see who has managed to find the most things from the list, and award that team a small prize.

At the end of the activity, see if there are any common themes among the religious stories or quotes that people found. Are people of faith presented positively or negatively? Is the church shown as a force of good (e.g. helping the homeless) or evil (e.g. child abuse scandals)? Let this discussion roll on if they've uncovered some interesting examples.

What's the purpose?

Possible learning/discussion points from this game:

- In the UK, we now live in a "post-Christian" culture, meaning we're no longer considered by most people to be a "Christian country". However, the media remain fascinated by the church and what it has to say – although how this is reported can vary wildly.

- The church is seen in a negative light by lots of people – especially militant atheists and secularists who are looking to limit its influence.

129. Keep going

Theme connection: Faith, perseverance

Age suitability: 11+

Resources needed: Water balloons, buckets of water, mop and clean-up kit

Venue requirements: Hold this game outside or in a place where you can make a splash without destroying any technical equipment!

Background preparation: None

The game

Split into two or more teams, and hold a relay race with a difference – the runners have to carry a water balloon… without using their hands.

Explain and demonstrate some of the ways they might choose to do this. They can either wedge, balance, or find some other innovative way of carrying the balloons back and forth.

Make sure you use cheap (weak) water balloons for maximum hilarity. If their balloon bursts while they're running, they have to go back and get another, although if the balloon bursts during the "handover" (which of course must not involve hands), let them off. The winning team is the first to have everyone complete a "leg" of the race.

What's the purpose?

Possible learning/discussion point from this game:

- It's one thing to fill a balloon with water; it's quite another to run with it. The same is true of faith – deciding to follow Jesus is just the start; it's possible that if we don't take our daily relationship with God seriously, things can still go wrong very quickly.

130. Back writing relay

Theme connection: Communication, truth

Age suitability: 9+

Resources needed: Some (simple) pictures for the teams to copy/draw

Venue requirements: None

Background preparation: Prepare some simple pictures for the teams to attempt to duplicate

The game

Divide your group into teams of about half a dozen or so, and get them lined up facing the front, as for a relay race. Give the person at the front of the line a pencil and piece of paper and explain that you are going to show a simple picture to the person at the back of the line. They then have to draw that picture onto the back of the person in front of them, that person then has to draw the picture they felt on their back onto the back of the person in front of them… and so on, until it reaches the person at the front. That person then draws what they think the picture is onto the sheet of paper. Reveal the correct image, and compare which team is the closest.

Repeat a couple of times, increasing the complexity of the pictures each time, and allowing different people to have a turn at being at the front.

What's the purpose?

Possible learning/discussion points from this game:

- How do you ensure that what you're trying to communicate is passed on faithfully?

- How do you know that you have got the message right yourself?

131. Binball

Theme connection: Waste, creation, justice
Age suitability: 7+
Resources needed: Two balls, a bin
Venue requirements: Enough space to run around a large circle
Background preparation: None

The game

Get your young people seated in a loose circle with a bin or suitably large receptacle containing two balls in the middle of the circle. Divide your circle into two halves (teams), numbering each team member counting from one upwards. When you call out a number, the two players with that number (one from each team) have to run to the middle, grab one of the balls, then exit the circle via where they had been sitting, and proceed to race round the circle in a clockwise direction (as we're writing this in the northern hemisphere, feel free to make a change if you're a youth worker of an Antipodean persuasion) until they get back to their spot, at which point they return their ball to the bin in the middle and sit down.

The first of the two to get the ball back in the bin and sit down wins a point for their team. Repeat until everyone has had a go.

Top tip: write down the numbers you have called so you can make sure that you a) don't forget anyone, and b) keep score.

What's the purpose?

Possible learning/discussion points from this game:

- Do you ever think about the things that you put into the bin? About what happens to it, or about how much you waste? Do you recycle?

- Should Christians take a lead in environmental campaigning? Why?

132. Would I not tell the truth to you?

Theme connection: Truth, lies, discernment

Age suitability: 14+

Resources needed: Three stools, statement cards

Venue requirements: None

Background preparation: Preselect three articulate and believable people who you know will enter into the spirit of the game (you may want to use volunteer leaders as your "contestants"). One of the volunteers will be telling the audience a true fact about themselves, so you will need to work this out in advance. Create three cue cards, with the two false statements below and this third true statement, ahead of the meeting.

The game

This game is based fairly directly on a popular TV panel show. Set up three stools at the front of your meeting, and invite your three contestants to sit on them. Give each of them one of three cards (this will be the first time they've seen them). The first two read:

- As a child, I just missed out on a place in the national under-11 synchronized modern tapdance finals after my partner fell off the stage.

- I am mildly allergic to methane, and have to move into another room if someone has passed wind.

The third statement is a true but obscure fact about your third contestant, and hopefully one which sounds like a lie. They read this card; now all three have to convince the group that theirs is the true statement, and that the other two are lying.

The rest of the group can ask questions – respectfully – and the panellists can choose whether and how to answer. Take a vote as a group as to who is really telling the truth, and then reveal who the liars were.

What's the purpose?

Possible learning/discussion points from this game:

- Sometimes discernment is difficult. People will seek to mislead us, and sometimes we'll need spiritual help to perceive what's really going on.

- There are lots of lies out there. Some of them are insignificant and silly; others are lies about what's important in life. When we talk about Jesus, we're talking about the real deal.

133. Prisonball

Theme connection: Sin, teamwork

Age suitability: 9+

Resources needed: Several foam balls

Venue requirements: A large open space (e.g. church hall)

Background preparation: Mark out a rectangular playing area along the length of a hall, with a divide (width-ways) across the middle, and with two clearly marked "prisons" that stretch across the width of the playing area, one at each end

The game

Divide your group into two teams and send one to each half of the playing area. Explain that this is "their" playing area, and that behind the opposition's playing area is "their" prison. They are not allowed to cross the lines in or out of these playing areas unless they are sent to, or released from, prison.

The aim of the game is to get all of the opposing team into prison at the same time. The way to do this is using the standard dodgeball technique of throwing a foam ball so it cleanly hits a member of the opposition below the waist, no rebounds/bounces allowed. (If needed you can make things tougher by only allowing hits below the knee.) Once a person is hit in this way, they are sent to their team's prison (behind the opposing team). Once they are there, they still remain active in the game. If one of the balls manages to get into the prison (make clear that they are not allowed out of the prison to fetch a ball, and nor are the opposition allowed into the prison to fetch one) they can regain their freedom by getting a member of the opposition out (again by hitting them below the waist in the normal dodgeball way). If they do this, they go back into the main playing area and the hit player has to go to their team's prison.

Begin the game by placing at least two foam balls on the dividing line across the middle, with all the players lined up on the back line of their playing area. Give the instruction to go and let the fun commence. Depending on player numbers/skill levels you might want to introduce more foam balls into the game, or to increase the mayhem. Keep playing until one of the teams has all its players in prison.

What's the purpose?

Possible learning/discussion points from this game:

- The Bible talks of Jesus setting us free from sin and the power of death – what does this actually mean?

- What do your group think about hell?

134. Alternative scoring

Theme connection: Grace, justice, fairness, teamwork

Age suitability: 9+

Resources needed: Football/basketball/Unihoc set (as applicable), flip chart, pens

Venue requirements: Enough space to play the game

Background preparation: Set up to play your group's favourite sports contest

The game

Less of a game in itself, but instead more of a technique that can be used to liven up any of the traditional sports games that your group might enjoy, e.g. football, Unihoc, volleyball (or even basketball if your set-up allows).

Simply introduce your game as normal but explain that when it comes to scoring, you will be using a different system – make sure they know that it is one which will be fair and consistent. Don't tell them any more at this stage, but suggest that any team which works it out will receive a bonus score at your discretion.

The system that you use is that instead of allocating points as normal, you award them based on the number of consecutive touches that team had before scoring. For example, if three players from Team A touch the ball before scoring (without the opposition touching it) give them three points, but if only one player touches it, then score just the single point. (For volleyball give the points for the number of touches the team has between them before hitting it successfully over the net.)

Make sure that you announce the scores clearly after each goal (be ready for protests when you do so!) and keep track of the scores on the flip chart clearly so everyone can see them. This is a great system for promoting teamwork and it can be continued once they've worked it out.

If the game you're employing this technique with normally has keepers, it may be worth removing them to allow for more scoring opportunities.

Also, if the idea of simply playing football/Unihoc, etc. is a bit passé for your group, why not make it more interesting by placing tables on their sides around the room to create a playing arena vibe? This works particularly effectively with Unihoc and three-a-side football tournaments in smaller spaces.

What's the purpose?

Possible learning/discussion points from this game:

- What is justice? What is fair?

- Is grace a "fair" concept?

135. Capture the Flag

Theme connection: Teamwork

Age suitability: 11+

Resources needed: Two "flags", cones to mark out playing area, whistle

Venue requirements: Large open space, preferably outdoors

Background preparation: Divide your playing area into two halves, with a line clearly separating them. Also mark out deep within each half a small prison area, and a "flag-base". In the centre of each flag base place some kind of flag (or any other alternative that seems to work – ranging from jumpers to teddy bears!)

The game

Divide your group into two equal teams, and gather them together for instructions. Explain that the aim of the game is to get the "flag" from their opponents' flag-base safely back to their own half without being tagged. If they are tagged they are sent to the prison in the opposition half and can only be freed by a teammate tagging them free (without being caught themselves!). If anyone is tagged whilst carrying the flag, the flag returns to its base before another team member can have a go at getting it back to their own half. Players aren't allowed into their own base, so once someone gets into the opposition base they are "safe"; however they still need to get the flag back into their own half to score. Players can only be tagged within the opposition half.

The game starts with each team in their own half and they can begin their moves when you blow the whistle. Once a team gets their flag back to their own half, blow your whistle to signify the end of the "play". The game may (certainly initially) be over quite quickly, so it's worth playing a few rounds of it – e.g. first team to five/ten/fifteen/100 dependent on how energetic your group is!

What's the purpose?

Possible learning/discussion points from this game:

- This game can only work if the team works together – how did this work out?

- Did they divide out roles? How did they decide who took what role?

136. Secret messages

Theme connection: Discernment, community, listening to God

Age suitability: 11+ (adaptable)

Resources needed: Pens, paper, copies of coded message (enough for one per group), flip chart/board/projector, lots of small chocolate prizes

Venue requirements: This game will work best in a quiet venue, ideally with surfaces on which to write

Background preparation: This is a code-cracking game. You can adapt this activity by setting your own code, appropriate to the age or ability levels you're working with. Before you start you will need to have established the code, created an obscure message in that code (see below for example), and chosen two keys to display on your flip chart

The game

Split into groups of no more than four, and hand out paper and pens, plus copies of your coded message. The message below is coded in such a way that each letter is represented by the number of its place in the alphabet PLUS five. So A=6, J=15, Z=31, and so on. Here's the example message:

10/9/9/14/10 – 12/14/23/6/11/11/10 – 28/10/6/23/24 – 18/6/24/24/14/27/10 – 21/6/19/25/24

… which translates as "Eddie Giraffe Wears Massive Pants" (deliberately obscure to stop them guessing).

On your flip chart paper, board, or projector, display the following keys only, which will hopefully help them to crack the code:

13=H
28=W

If they're really stuck, you could give them one or two of the letters which actually appear in the message.

Give prizes to all the groups who crack the code, with double prizes for the team which finishes first. If you want to extend the activity, ask them to write a message back to you using the same code.

What's the purpose?

Possible learning/discussion points from this game:

- It's not always easy to discern God's voice and plan for our lives; sometimes it needs a bit of work from us to think and translate what he might be saying to us.

- Discernment isn't always an individual activity; we can help other Christians to work out what God might be saying to them – this is one of the many functions of being church.

137. Toilet Paper Mummy

Theme connection: History, Bible

Age suitability: 9+

Resources needed: Toilet paper (two rolls per three members of your group)

Venue requirements: None

Background preparation: None

The game

Divide your group up into threes and give each team two rolls of toilet paper. Get them to decide among themselves who is to become an Ancient Egyptian Mummy and then give them five minutes to turn that individual into the best approximation of a mummy possible, using only toilet paper. Judge the entries on effort, attention to detail, and of course creativity.

What's the purpose?

Possible learning/discussion points from this game:

- "History is important". Discuss.

- The narrative of the people of Israel being freed from slavery in Egypt (the Exodus) is a key concept in the Bible. Where are some of the places in the rest of the Bible that your group can spot connections and echoes of this liberation?

138. Chair Dodgeball

Theme connection: Avoidance

Age suitability: 9+

Resources needed: Some form of dividing marker, a number of foam balls (at least two), eight chairs

Venue requirements: A large playing space (e.g. a church hall)

Background preparation: Divide the hall into two halves, mark out the dividing line, and place four chairs, evenly spaced, at each end

The game

Split your group into even teams and send one team to each half of the hall, placing the foam balls into starting position on the line along the middle of the hall. Explain that the aim of the game is to fill the four chairs at the end of your half with opposition members. The way to do this is in classic dodgeball style: restricted to their half of the hall, the players throw the balls and try to hit opposing team members directly (no rebounds) below the knee.

Once a player is hit, they have to go and stand on one of the chairs behind their opposition. Once all four chairs are filled, the team in front of them wins. The people on the chairs can however release themselves by catching a ball thrown by one of their teammates from within their own half – if they manage to catch the ball, then they can rejoin their teammates, and the game proceeds until one of the sets of chairs is filled. You will need to referee carefully to see when players have been hit, and check when the chairs are filled.

What's the purpose?

Possible learning/discussion points from this game:

- Ask your group: if they could pick one issue that they will never have to confront for the rest of their lives, what would it be and why?

- Use this game as a way in to talking about any issue that young people (or the church) might traditionally "dodge".

139. Ping pong ball racing

Theme connection: Influence on the world

Age suitability: 9+

Resources needed: Ping pong balls, chairs/boxes/tables/ assorted junk to make a slalom course, straws (optional)

Venue requirements: None

Background preparation: Construct two simple, short (equal) slalom courses using chairs/boxes/tables

The game

Divide your group in half and line up a team at the start of each course. Explain that their task is for each team member to propel a ping pong ball along the slalom course, using only their breath. Demonstrate how easy it is to blow a ping pong ball around and clearly state that anyone caught touching their ping pong ball will be sent back to the start of the course.

Give each team a ball, get them lined up, and start the race. The winning team is the first to have all their members successfully take a turn at blowing the ping pong ball around the course and return to the start line.

To make it more of a focused and skill-based race, give each player a straw to blow the ping pong ball round with. Keep a close eye out for any "touching".

What's the purpose?

Possible learning/discussion points from this game:

- Ping pong balls are easy to control, but what areas of life do your group want to have an effect on?

- What areas do they feel like they cannot control?

140. Scrap paper wars

Theme connection: Recycling, war, creation

Age suitability: 9+

Resources needed: Scrap paper, a whistle (optional)

Venue requirements: A large space, e.g. a hall

Background preparation: Collect as much scrap paper as possible and divide it into two equal piles

The game

You're bound to have some scrap paper lying around your meeting space (sermons, old Bible studies, important permission letters that never got taken home, etc.) so instead of simply recycling it, why not use it for one final glorious hurrah (if paper had emotions, that's exactly how it would view this game) before filling up your recycling box?

Simply divide the paper between two teams, and equally divide your space into two halves – one for each team. Send each team to "their half" and explain that you'll give them one minute (or as appropriate dependent on your quantity of paper!) to prepare the "ammunition" by crumpling it into balls, folding it into planes (or however they choose), and then you'll give them another minute to try and throw as much paper into their opponent's half as possible, while simultaneously trying to remove any that lands in their own half. Time, and announce clearly, the minutes and make sure they stop throwing/flicking the paper as soon as you indicate it's over (hint: a whistle might be useful!).

Make sure they know it's a non-contact game (!) and that any throwing/flicking paper after the time limit will be penalized. If you have the energy for it, gather and divide the paper again, and repeat!

If you don't have a massive amount of paper then simply downsize! Seat your group around a large clear table, and divide that into two, or mark out a space on your floor to use as the limits, and get your group sitting around that.

What's the purpose?

Possible learning/discussion points from this game:

- When something is finished with, is your instinct to see how you can reuse it, or to bin it?

- Do you consider your lifestyle to be environmentally friendly or not?

- War is one of the most destructive effects of the Fall and has massively messed up our planet over the past 100 years in particular. What part can you play in stopping war and living in peace?

141. Human tic-tac-toe

Theme connection: Planning ahead, awareness
Age suitability: 9+
Resources needed: Nine chairs
Venue requirements: Enough space for nine chairs to be set out
Background preparation: Set out the chairs in a three by three grid

The game

Divide your group into two teams. (You will need five players per team ideally – if you have many more than that, you could get a couple of games going simultaneously, or run it as a tournament so each team plays each other.) Each team takes it in turn for one of its players to sit in one of the nine seats, with the goal of getting a line of three players from the same team (as in noughts and crosses/tic-tac-toe).

The tricky thing is, of course, remembering who is on your team – so keep a close eye on which team is the first to achieve this. Play a number of times (e.g. best of five games) and ensure that the players take it in turns to go first on each team, so that the same player doesn't always get stuck missing their go at the end.

What's the purpose?

Possible learning/discussion point from this game:

- "Awareness" is essential in this game – do your group feel "aware" of God? What does it mean to become more aware of him in our daily lives?

142. Jaffa Cake jelly

Theme connection: What really matters, essentials

Age suitability: 9+

Resources needed: Plenty of packets of Jaffa Cakes, set of weighing scales (as sensitive as possible)

Venue requirements: None

Background preparation: None

The game

Divide your group into teams, and give each team several packets of chocolate-orange cake/biscuits (cheaper, non-branded alternatives may well be your friend budget-wise, and are just as effective). Explain that the competition is to eat the biscuit and chocolate, and to leave as much jelly as possible.

Collect each team's jelly innards and weigh them to work out who has the most jelly. Let the group know that you will be really strict on removing any bits of jelly which have chocolate or sponge still attached.

What's the purpose?

Possible learning/discussion points from this game:

- The jelly is essential to a Jaffa Cake, so what's really essential to your group?

- What are some things that you can and can't separate? In life? In the Christian faith?

143. Team lies

Theme connection: Lies, truth, community

Age suitability: 11+

Resources needed: None

Venue requirements: None

Background preparation: None

The game

This game (predictably) involves teams telling a lie and then working as a team to determine which of the things the other teams say is true and which are made-up.

Divide your group into pairs. Instruct each team that they need to come up with two facts about themselves <u>as a collective team</u>, one of which must be made-up. Encourage them to chat and get to know each other at this stage, and produce as outlandish facts as possible. (For example they could claim that collectively as a team they had lived on every continent on earth, that between them they owed two-thirds of the gross national debt of Greece, and that between them they have thirteen limbs.)

Each team gets an opportunity, one at a time, to share their facts about themselves, and once all the teams have had a chance to share the other teams have the task of deciding which of the facts is false. To aid them in this, each team is allowed to ask one question of each other team. The team has to answer the question truthfully if it is about either of the truths, but they are allowed to continue the fabrication if it's about their collective lie.

Each team should then write down what they think the lie is for each of the other teams, before you reveal the answers.

Give each team ten points for each of the lies they correctly identify in the other teams, and then a further ten points for each time any other team incorrectly identifies their own lie.

What's the purpose?

Possible learning/discussion points from this game:

- Do you find it easy to persuade someone of something, regardless of whether it's true or not? Does the issue of its truth make a difference?

- Sharing our story can be a powerful thing – do you ever share your story, or allow others to share their story with you?

144. Youth Group Top Trumps

Theme connection: Skill, identity

Age suitability: 11+

Resources needed: Enough pre-prepared "blank" Top Trump cards for each member of your group, pens, a coin to decide the starting team, any measuring equipment that might be needed (optional)

Venue requirements: None

Background preparation: Print off an appropriate number of blank Top Trump cards on pieces of A4 paper. Include space for name, and a small picture, and then come up with seven categories. Include some factual ones (e.g. age, shoe size, number of siblings, height, etc.) as well as more abstract ones (e.g. number of tall buildings leaped in a single bound, number of pianos that can be balanced on a finger, most treehouses built, etc.)

The game

As the young people arrive, get them to fill in a Top Trump card for themselves, with names and most importantly with "scores" in each category (if there's time get them to draw themselves on the card as well). Make the cards look as professional as possible with boxes for the answers. Give any help needed as to the actual answers (e.g. provide tape measures to check height) as well as providing some guidelines if necessary to help fill in answers in the abstract categories (e.g. offer a range of numbers from within which the players can choose their scores).

Divide your group into two teams, giving each player a random Top Trump card, and get the two teams to play off against each other. Get them lined up, and instruct the two front people of each team to step forward and face each other. Toss a coin to see which team gets to start and allow the player from that team to pick which category to compare scores in. Whichever team has the higher score (aka the higher number in this variation of the game) in that category wins, and both players go to the back of the line of the winning team.

The next two players step forward, and the player from the team which won the last round picks a category to compare scores as before, with both players going to the back of the queue of the winning team and so on... Keep going until one team has all the players, or until an impasse is reached!

What's the purpose?

Possible learning/discussion points from this game:

- What are the key elements of your identity?

- What superhero ability would you like to have?

145. Skittle Sort

Theme connection: Appearance, identity, discrimination

Age suitability: 9+

Resources needed: One big bowl, Skittles (the sweets), a straw for each player, an empty bowl per team

Venue requirements: None

Background preparation: Put the Skittles into the large bowl. You can have as many teams as there are different colours in the packet of Skittles, although don't feel the need to use all the colours unless numbers absolutely dictate – having a spare colour which no one wants to collect adds an element of challenge. Important: ensure that your straws aren't wide enough to suck a Skittle right up into the mouth!

The game

The aim of the game is for teams to collect as many Skittles of their allocated colour as possible using their straws and the power of suction.

Divide your group into equal-sized teams and place an empty bowl for each team at one end of your hall/playing space. Place the bowl with all the Skittles in it at the other end of the hall, equally accessible to all the teams, and get your teams to line up by their empty bowls.

If your group is small enough (anything under a dozen) you could allow them to go for the Skittles all at the same time, and the ensuing chaos becomes part of the challenge of the game. Otherwise, get your teams into lines and allow team members to go up one at a time in a relay manner, and, only using the straws, attempt to pick up an appropriately coloured Skittle and transport it back to the team's bowl. Any Skittle that falls off a straw is counted out of the game (and safely removed from under the feet by a helpful leader), and the player must return to their team and allow the next player to go up and have an attempt.

After an appropriate length of time call an end to the fetching, and count up how many Skittles each team has in their bowl. Subtract one for each incorrect colour that has been collected.

What's the purpose?

Possible learning/discussion point from this game:

- This could lead into a discussion on differences between people, and issues of appearance, identity, and discrimination.

146. There is No Spoon

Theme connection: Sharing, greed, justice

Age suitability: 9+

Resources needed: Five spoons, three chairs

Venue requirements: Enough space to run energetically, e.g. a church hall

Background preparation: Place three chairs equidistant from each other in a triangle (far enough apart to allow for running between) and place the five spoons on one of the chairs

The game

Divide your group into two groups and send each group to one of the two chairs without the spoons on them (it doesn't matter which as they should be equidistant!).

Explain that the aim of the game is simply to gather three spoons at your team's chair. Each team nominates one player to play a round. Those players take position at their team's base/chair, and at the start of the game they are allowed to run and fetch a spoon, and return it to their base. The only rules are that you can only carry one spoon at a time, and you can only pick up a spoon that is on one of the chairs (i.e. you can't take them from someone's hand). Other than that, you can take a spoon from either the main repository or your opponent's chair, but as long as there are less than three spoons on a chair the game continues...

Once a player gets three spoons back to their base their team wins that round, and each team nominates a new player to play the next round. Proceed until everyone has had a turn, totalling up the scores to find a winner.

What's the purpose?

Possible learning/discussion point from this game:

- Wouldn't the world be so much better if we all just shared? Is this possible or just an unrealistic dream?

147. Polo relay

Theme connection: Community, sharing

Age suitability: 9+

Resources needed: Enough toothpicks for everybody, two full packs of Polo mints, two empty dessert bowls

Venue requirements: None

Background preparation: None

The game

Get your group into two equal teams, give each member a toothpick, and get them to stand in a line, one behind the other. At the front of the line place a full pack of Polo mints, and at the end of the line place an empty dessert bowl.

Explain to the group that it's a team race where they compete to be the first to transfer all the Polos from the packet at the front to the bowl at the end of the line. The rules are simply that the Polos can only be moved one at a time by toothpick, that those toothpicks must be held in the mouth (no hands allowed), and the Polo must be passed along by every member of the team before being deposited in the bowl.

The person at the front is allowed to hold the Polo packet in their hands, and open it – but the Polo must be placed onto the toothpick without being touched, and it must then be passed onto the toothpick of the person behind, still without being touched, and so on. Once the person at the back has deposited the Polo in the bowl (still without touching it) they shout out "Polo", so the person at the front knows to start another Polo on its journey. Once the final mint is in the bowl the team sits down and shouts out "We've got the (w)hole packet in the bowl!"

Any dropped Polos have to continue their journey, but of course must be picked up from the ground without being touched by anything other than the toothpick held in the mouth!

If the journey of the Polo to the back of the teams is taking too long (perhaps because you have larger teams, or the task is proving tricky), you could allow a new Polo to be started off once the previous one passes the midpoint of the line.

What's the purpose?

Possible learning/discussion point from this game:

- Passing things to one another requires consideration of each other (and our relative toothpick skills) – does this come naturally to us?

148. Body Dice

Theme connection: Connections, sex, appropriate behaviour

Age suitability: 11+

Resources needed: A dice

Venue requirements: Enough space for people to stand in groups of six and make weird shapes with their bodies

Background preparation: None

The game

Divide your group into teams of six and spread them out across your meeting space, ensuring that there is plenty of space between teams.

The teams will be playing against each other in an effort to be the team that follows the instructions and survives the longest. Explain that they need to number each of their players from one through to six, and that that will be their number for the rest of the game. You as leader will roll the dice to find out which team member is in play, and then again to find out which body part they need to use – where the number one = elbow, two = armpit, three = ear, four = knee, five = foot, six = nose.

You then roll the dice again to find out the next team member needed, and once more to find out which body part they need to connect to the body part of the first teammate. For example, if you roll a six, followed by a five, and then a three followed by a four, it means Player Six has to attach their foot to Player Three's knee. They then have to hold this position, as well as obeying any further instructions they receive whenever their number is rolled again.

Keep on going, identifying pairs of players and which body parts they need to connect, so that each team ends up with a mixture of bizarre and tangled interconnections. If a body part already in play comes up again, they simply detach the original instruction and swap to the latest one – give the players the choice as to whether the left or right elbow/armpit/ear/knee/foot is used each time. Keep going until all of the teams are unable to maintain structural integrity and/ or balance!

It goes without saying that you will need to be careful to keep this appropriate! Except that we've said it now. Either way, make sure you're aware.

What's the purpose?

Possible learning/discussion point from this game:

- Did they find this game awkward? Why/why not? Other topics discussed will depend on the age group.

149. Islands

Theme connection: Journeying, teamwork, planning ahead

Age suitability: 9+

Resources needed: Chalk or masking tape

Venue requirements: A hall, and a floor that you can mark

Background preparation: Mark on the floor lots of "islands" (masking tape or chalk both work, dependent on your floor surface). These shapes need to be close enough together that people can move from one to another without necessarily having to be long-jump experts, and of a size that it is not easy for two people to pass each other without stepping off. They should be placed liberally about the hall so that it is possible to get from one end of the hall to the other on these islands.

The game

Divide your group into two teams and start each team at opposite ends of the hall. Explain that the aim of the game is for the whole team to get from one end of the hall to the other without stepping out of an island (into the "sea") and without touching a member of the opposite team. The winning team is the first to get all their team members to the other side.

Each team takes it in turns for one player to move one step – this can be a small step or a large leap, but they have to land cleanly within an island. If they overbalance, or take another step to steady themselves, or put a hand/foot outside of the island, they have to go back to the start. Equally, if they touch a member of the other team in this move then they must again go back to the beginning (although opposition team members are not allowed to deliberately thrust arms/hands/legs out to ensure that they are touched!).

Get each team to nominate a captain who makes the final decision over who makes a move each turn – allow discussion about moves to occur, but keep the game moving by putting a time limit on each move (you could put more pressure on this as the two teams come closer to each other!).

This is a game of teamwork and strategy, so allow some time at the start of each game for the teams to discuss their tactics.

What's the purpose?

Possible learning/discussion point from this game:

- What "journeys" are the young people on? Are they intentionally planning where they are going, or simply responding to each thing as it comes?

150. Three-legged five-a-side

Theme connection: Teamwork

Age suitability: 9+

Resources needed: Tables, a football, string/wool/scarves to tie pairs of ankles together

Venue requirements: A hall

Background preparation: Turn your hall into a five-a-side arena by placing tables on their sides around the edges of the room with a gap at each end for goals

The game

Divide your group into randomly allocated pairs. Tie the pairs together at the ankle (as you would for a three-legged race) and then get the pairs into teams. Depending on the size of your playing arena, you'll probably want three pairs per team (unless you have a really good-sized hall, five-a-side is probably just a wistfully optimistic title), and then get the teams to play each other in short matches of two minutes.

Allow no goalies, or above head height passes/shots, and keep the games rolling. Play each team against each other and keep track of the final scores to create a mini-league table. Alternatively, if there are too many teams to realistically do this, you could hold a knockout cup competition.

What's the purpose?

Possible learning/discussion points from this game:

- "The value of cooperation" – discuss.

- Which professional footballers would be best/worst at this if this was how real football was played?

- Are footballers fairly paid or overpaid (considering the millions they generate for their clubs)?

151. Malteser Mush

Theme connection: Redemption

Age suitability: 11+

Resources needed: Maltesers, straws, a bowl of "gloop" per team (see below), an empty bowl/plate per team, stopwatch (optional)

Venue requirements: A space where it won't matter if Maltesers/ gloop end up on the floor (not carpeted)

Background preparation: For this game you will need to create an edible and gungy mush or "gloop" in a large bowl. (Think baked beans, mushy peas – any sauce-based foodstuff will do, but make sure you're aware of any potential allergy issues.)

The game

Get your group into equal teams of up to eight, providing each team with a bowl of gloop, and each player with a straw. Explain that you are going to stir a packet of Maltesers into the gloop, and that their task is to remove these using only the straws, their mouths, and the power of suction (it might be worth demonstrating how easy it is to move a Malteser by sucking one end of the straw and picking a sweet up).

In full view of the group, carefully stir into each bowl a packet of Maltesers (making sure that there are plenty more Maltesers in each bowl than team members), pushing them under the surface of the liquid as much as possible. Provide each team with an empty plate/ bowl to put the retrieved Maltesers in. Once this is done, on your count allow the teams to begin retrieving the sweets.

This game works best as a relay, with only one team member at a time trying to remove a sweet, but if your groups are small (two or three per team) they could all try to find and remove the sweets at the same time for added chaotic fun.

If you have counted how many Maltesers went into the gloop you could simply set a target number of sweets to be removed, or alternatively set a time limit and declare the winners to be the team who have managed to remove the most Maltesers in that time.

What's the purpose?

Possible learning/discussion point from this game:

- The idea of good things coming out of the bad is a reminder of the redeeming work of Jesus – (how) do they experience this in everyday life?

152. Build a Tower

Theme connection: Creativity

Age suitability: 7+

Resources needed: Piles of newspaper, a roll of sticky tape per team, tape measure (or some other means of measuring the finished towers)

Venue requirements: None

Background preparation: Divide your newspaper into equal piles for each team

The game

Divide your group into teams of three to four, and give each team some flat space, an equal pile of newspaper, and a single roll of sticky tape.

Explain that their task is to create the tallest free-standing newspaper tower possible (i.e. one that doesn't lean on anything, or isn't supported by anything other than the newspaper that you provide). It's down to your discretion (and floor covering) as to whether you allow the teams to anchor the bottom of the tower to the floor by taping it down. Give the teams a time limit (for example, of no more than seven minutes) to complete their tower, then allow everyone to walk around and look at each other's creations, art gallery style, at the end.

What's the purpose?

Possible learning/discussion points from this game:

- Do your young people think of themselves as creative?

- What do they think of the idea that as God made us in his own image, we all share his characteristic of creativity as part of our existence?

153. Newspaper Hockey

Theme connection: Recycling, longevity

Age suitability: 7+

Resources needed: Plenty of newspaper and sticky tape, two chairs

Venue requirements: Plenty of space, preferably a hall with an uncarpeted floor

Background preparation: Make some "ice-hockey" pucks out of newspaper and sticky tape (these should be discs of paper about 5 cm thick, tightly bound together with tape, ideally with two flat and smooth sides)

The game

Divide your group into two equal teams, and give each team a pile of newspapers and some tape, along with the instructions that they need to use these to make a number of "hockey" sticks. Explain that they can make as many or as few as they like, but that they should ensure that the sticks are as sturdy and durable as possible.

Once the teams have finished constructing their sticks, fetch your pre-prepared pucks, and get the two teams sitting down on opposite sides of the hall. Individually number the players, counting up from one on each team so that you end up with a player on each team numbered one, a player on each team numbered two, etc.

Place a chair at each end of the hall and explain that the aim of the game is to score a goal by hitting the puck between the chair legs. Place one of your carefully constructed pucks in the exact centre of the hall, between the two teams, and explain that you are going to call out a number at random. The two players with that number have to grab one of the sticks that their team has made (pile them up by each team) and then try to be the first player to score by hitting the puck into their goal (make sure that your teams know which goal each is aiming for!). Once a goal is scored the pair goes to sit down, you reset the puck, and call out another number.

Crucially, though, play will only continue as long as each team has a viable "stick" that they can play with – once a team has exhausted all the sticks they've made, the game is over. You then add up the total scores, awarding a bonus goal for each remaining stick to the team that made them, to find your winners.

What's the purpose?

Possible learning/discussion points from this game:

- Do they value things that last?

- Do you repair things, or tend to throw away even the things that could be repaired? What do you think our semi-disposable lifestyles say about us as a culture?

154. M&M move

Theme connection: Overcoming challenges, perseverance, identity

Age suitability: 9+

Resources needed: Enough toothpicks for everybody to have two each, a large bowl, a large packet (or two) of M&Ms or similar, empty bowls for each team

Venue requirements: A large room/hall

Background preparation: Put the M&Ms into the large bowl and place it in the centre of your hall. Check for food allergies

The game

Equally divide your group into as many teams as there are different colours of M&Ms (or some such other small, rounded, multicoloured confectionery such as Skittles, Smarties, Mini Eggs, etc). and pour a big bag or two of your chosen confectionery into a big bowl in the middle of the room. Give each team an empty bowl, placed at an equal distance from the central bowl in different parts of the room, and enough toothpicks for each team member to have two.

Explain that this is less of a game than a generous move on your part to allow the group to consume some sweets, but that you want them to earn their reward by demonstrating a level of skill, dexterity, and cultural awareness. Giving each team a colour of sweet to target, tell them that at the end of each round they get to eat all the sweets of that colour that they have managed to transfer from the central bowl to their team bowl, with the rule being that they can only transport one sweet at a time, and it has to be done using only the toothpicks. They can use these in a chopstick-style, or holding one in each hand as a poor imitation of a knife and fork, but they cannot touch the sweets with their hands (or any other body part).

Give them a bit of time to practise their toothpick skills, before giving them thirty seconds to collect as many of their coloured sweets as they can. At the end of the time check their stash, and for each one of the wrong colour that they have collected, take away one of their target sweets. Finally count up how many each team has collected before letting them consume their stash.

It may be worth repeating this a number of times, each time swapping the colours around, so that the teams are trying to collect different colours each time (but you will obviously need to replenish your supply of sweets!). Continue until you run out of sweets, or the group no longer want to eat any more (!)...

What's the purpose?

Possible learning/discussion point from this game:

- Perseverance is the key here, so use this game as a discussion starter to talk about the biblically backed virtue. Why is perseverance a good thing? Do the young people think it's something that many people possess these days – and if so, what are some great cultural examples or stories of it that they can draw on?

155. Bags of Rubbish

Theme connection: Waste, recycling, evangelism

Age suitability: 7+

Resources needed: Black bin bag per team, newspaper per team

Venue requirements: None

Background preparation: None

The game

Divide your group into teams as big or small as you like. Give each team a black bag and an equal-sized newspaper, and explain to them that their task is to make their black bag the biggest it can be (with the widest circumference, and as tall as possible). Make sure they know that by crumpling up individual sheets loosely, they can make larger balls of newspaper and by fitting them carefully into the bag, they can optimize its size. Give them a time limit for this (e.g. three minutes – dependent on the amount of newspaper) and at the end of it judge the bags, putting them into order of size. Award one point to the last- placed team, two points to the team above them, and so on…

Then announce there is another part of the competition – where they have to compress their bags of newspaper to make them as small as possible. Leave them to work out their favourite technique for themselves, but again give them a time limit to complete this in. Compare the sizes of the bags to see which is the smallest, again putting them all into order and awarding points from last place (one point) up to first place, before declaring the winners to be the team with the most points across the two parts of the competition.

Finally place all the newspaper into the recycling.

Tip: Alternatively, you can play this as a follow-on from another game involving a certain amount of rubbish. In that case, take Mary Poppins' advice, and make a game of the clearing up, giving each team a rubbish bag, and award a prize to the team with the fullest bag.

What's the purpose?

Possible learning/discussion points from this game:

- The big, puffed-up bags contained the same amount of newspaper as the small, compressed versions. So is it better to do something small with a concentrated effect, or something big with a less powerful impact? You could use this as a way to talk about approaches to Christian mission/evangelism. Is it better to be deep or wide?

- Do you recycle? Is there more you can do?

- Start a discussion about simplifying your life; where could you have less or give things away?

156. Human Skittles

Theme connection: Knocking down, building
Age suitability: 9+
Resources needed: A foam ball
Venue requirements: A long room
Background preparation: None

The game

Divide your group into two equal teams and send each to one end of your hall. Get one team to arrange themselves into a triangle formation with the point facing towards the opposing team (like an arrangement of bowling pins), spread out about an arm's length apart from each other. They will be the pins at which the opposing team will try to aim. Give the opposing team a (foam!) ball and a line from behind which to "bowl" and get them to try to get all the pins down. Get them to take it in turns to bowl until all the pins are down.

Obviously you won't be actually knocking the "pins" over, simply hitting them will do, but ensure that the ball is bowled (i.e. rolled underarm) rather than thrown. Keep a close eye out for rebounds, and eliminate every "hit" pin (move them out of the pin formation, leaving the remaining pins where they are) after each bowl. Record how many shots it takes to remove all the pins.

Once the first team has bowled all the pins over, swap the team roles over so that the second team is now bowling at the first. Repeat as necessary to allow each group member plenty of opportunity to bowl and stand in different positions in the triangle – ensure each team has an equal number of opportunities to bowl and be bowled at, and award the victory to the team with the lowest total number of bowls taken to bowl out the opposition.

What's the purpose?

Possible learning/discussion points from this game:

- People often say "It's easier to knock down than to build up" – why?

- How easy or difficult do your group find it to encourage one another?

157. Chinese Dragon

Theme connection: Spiritual attack, perseverance
Age suitability: 9+
Resources needed: A foam ball
Venue requirements: None
Background preparation: None

The game

Pick half a dozen people from your group and get them to stand with their hands on the shoulders of the person in front of them (forming a Chinese-style dragon) and tell the rest of the group to form a loose circle around them. The aim of the game is for the group to eliminate the dragon; they do so by hitting the person at the back of the dragon (as we all know Chinese dragons are most vulnerable at their tail) with a (foam) ball (as we all know the natural foe of the Chinese dragon is the foam ball).

The dragon needs to try to stay alive for as long as possible by preventing the ball from hitting the person at the back of the dragon – the "head" of the dragon can use their arms to deflect the ball and so on, and by moving about quickly they should be able to keep the tail fairly well protected. If the person at the back is hit by the ball then they are eliminated and join the circle, and the person who was in front of them obviously becomes the new tail (as we all know Chinese dragons grow new tails very quickly) which needs to be hit/defended, and so on until the whole dragon is defeated. At this stage pick some new volunteers to become the next dragon.

The group will hopefully develop techniques of passing the ball around the circle – if this is not happening be prepared to give hints. If the group is larger you can make the dragon larger (or smaller) as appropriate.

What's the purpose?

Possible learning/discussion points from this game:

- How do you respond when you're under attack?

- What do you think about the idea of being under attack spiritually?

158. Four on a sofa

Theme connection: Gender, sexism, identity

Age suitability: 11+

Resources needed: Paper, pens, a sofa (or four demarcated chairs), enough chairs for everybody else

Venue requirements: Enough space to seat your group on chairs in a circle

Background preparation: Before the game get everybody to write their names on pieces of paper

The game

Shuffle the names on the pieces of paper and hand them out so that everybody has someone else's name. Get everyone sitting in a circle with one empty space and four special seats (this can be the eponymous sofa, or in the absence of a large enough sofa simply four chairs marked out in some way will suffice). Make sure that there are two girls and two boys sitting on the "sofa". The aim of the game is for the "boys'" team to fill the sofa with boys, and for the girls to fill the spaces with girls. They make this happen in the following way:

Get the person sitting on the right of the empty space to say the name of someone in the group, and whoever has that name on their piece of paper has to come and sit in the empty seat. The person who is now on the right of the newly vacated space then gets to call out a name, and whoever has that name comes to sit there… and so on.

As they keep track of who is who, and where they are sitting, they will begin to work out a strategy. Or alternatively play on in a trial and error manner until they get lucky! Remind the boys that their target is to get a sofa full of guys, and the girls that they're trying to fill the sofa with girls.

This game doesn't work well with too big a group – or obviously with too small a group either, but with up to twenty or so this game is a great way to get them thinking, and working, as a team.

What's the purpose?

Possible learning/discussion points from this game:

- What's their perception of sexism in the world?

- Do the girls expect to be favoured/discriminated against by members of their sex? What about the boys?

- Do they feel an allegiance to their gender?

10

Small Group Games

If there's one group of people who are most likely to find this book frustrating, it's youth leaders working with a small group. Complex large-scale games and relay obstacle courses are all well and good, but what if you've only got three young people? If that's you, we hope this chapter of games aimed specifically at smaller groups will alleviate any sense of rising anger created by the previous nine.

> *Yup, nothing more frustrating than reading about*
> *a great idea for a game, and then realizing that it's*
> *based on having enough players to fill a ten thousand*
> *seater stadium. Or even having a ten thousand seater*
> *stadium.*

First of all, let us say without any sense of condescension that if you're running a small youth group, we salute you. Sustaining a small group can involve a lot of work, while looking to grow larger can pose all sorts of challenges, not least because your group will have such a strong sense of identity that it can feel difficult for outsiders to integrate. These games are all designed to ensure that your group's size doesn't prevent it from being a fun place to be, both for regulars and for any new recruits.

> *Another point is that some games are easier/better*
> *with smaller groups, so even if you have a large group,*
> *it may be worth on occasions breaking into smaller*
> *groups for games. This is particularly important if you*

have some individuals who might struggle with larger-scale activities, as doing games in small groups can give them an opportunity to participate in a way they otherwise may be excluded from. Think small, but think inclusive!

These games would also all be suitable for use in a "cell group" context, if your youth work involves such things.

159. Object balloon debate

Theme connection: Materialism, consumerism

Age suitability: 14+

Resources needed: Set of object cards for each group (pieces of paper/card, each with one of the following printed on them: Xbox, TV, computer, heavy Bible, CD player and CDs, journal and art materials, case full of designer clothes, mountain bike, etc.)

Venue requirements: None

Background preparation: Create the sets of eight cards listed above, and set out your venue so that groups of six to eight can sit in circles

The game

This game works best in groups of six to eight young people, so if you have more than that, split into small groups, placing a leader/helper with each group if you can.

Give each group a set of object cards – group members take one each. Now explain that the groups are in an imaginary hot air balloon. The balloon is in trouble and is going to crash, as in the classic "balloon debate" game, unless one of the objects is thrown overboard.

Each person has to "become" the object on their card (they have to imagine that inanimate objects can think, talk, and throw themselves out of hot air balloons!) and defend their right to stay on board. Each group member gets thirty seconds to make their case as to why they're important to the imaginary pilot of the balloon; after everyone has spoken, the group members take a vote on who/what gets thrown overboard.

Some extra information in case you have a pedantic group:

- The balloon belongs to the pilot, who doesn't have any money to replace any of their treasured possessions once they're gone.

- The objects all weigh roughly the same.

Once they've agreed, spring a surprise on them – they now have to do it again. If time allows and the activity is going well, keep going until you only have one or two objects left on each balloon.

What's the purpose?

Possible learning/discussion points from this game:

- There's a difference between the things that we want and the things that we need; this activity helps us to draw the distinction.

- Our consumerist culture draws us into believing that we need all these things to be happy, but in fact none of these things satisfy us (except perhaps for the Bible!).

160. The Chocolate Game

Theme connection: Teamwork, justice

Age suitability: 9+

Resources needed: One big bar of chocolate, a large plate, a knife and fork, a pair of dice, a variety of outdoor wear (hat, scarf, gloves, etc.)

Venue requirements: None

Background preparation: None

The game

Get the young people to sit in a circle with the chocolate (unwrapped but still unbroken) on the plate with the knife and fork and garments in the middle. Take it in turns to roll the dice – and as soon as someone rolls a pair of sixes, they get to put on the hat/gloves/scarf and eat as much chocolate as they can using only the knife and fork. While they do this, the rolling of the dice progresses around the circle. As soon as someone else gets a double six, the person in the middle has to stop and pass on the clothes/cutlery to the new person. Play until the chocolate is gone.

Make the chocolate as large as it needs to be for your group (a 200g or 400g bar should do the trick depending on the size of group) and feel free to vary the clothing requirements as allowed by your sense of humour/whatever you have cluttering up your office! Perhaps theme it depending on the time of year – e.g. swimming hat, goggles, towel round the neck, etc. in summer? It is also worth being aware of the likelihood of disappointed young people who got no turns to guzzle any chocolate – a spare bar can sometimes be a demonstration of grace in this situation!

What's the purpose?

Possible learning/discussion points from this game:

- Did anyone not get as much chocolate as the rest of the group – is this fair?

- How did it feel watching someone else eating all the chocolate before you had a chance to? Is this anything like life?

161. Human Knot

Theme connection: Connections

Age suitability: 9+

Resources needed: None

Venue requirements: None

Background preparation: None

The game

Get your group to form a circle, and then instruct them to put their hands into the centre of the circle and grab any other two hands at random. Their task is then to "untangle" the knot without letting go of hands. This task will not always be possible, so expect to repeat this process a few times, particularly as once they get the hang of it, they will want to do it again.

Be warned that while this can be done as a competitive exercise between two similarly sized groups, adding the element of speed will increase the likelihood of twisted arms, as the more enthusiastic members of the groups seek to untangle quickly. (Also beware of any Classics students who suggest an Alexandrian approach to untying the Gordian knot. Forbid this in the strongest possible terms!)

What's the purpose?

Possible learning/discussion point from this game:

* We're constantly told about the increased connections we all have with each other because of things like social media, but does this make life better? Does it make it easier? Does it make any difference?

162. The Peg Game

Theme connection: Connections, materialism, sin

Age suitability: 9+

Resources needed: Plenty of clothes pegs (about twenty per person), stopwatch

Venue requirements: None

Background preparation: None

The game

Give each young person a number of pegs (about twenty is ideal – but simply adapt your game length if you have less) and after carefully instructing your group where it is appropriate to peg each other (!) give them two minutes to get rid of their pegs by pegging them onto other people, while simultaneously avoiding being pegged oneself. At the end of the two minutes, count who has the fewest pegs attached to them to find a winner.

What's the purpose?

Possible learning/discussion points from this game:

- What do you feel attached to?

- What do you feel attaches itself to you that you might not want, or might not be helpful?

163. Up Jenkins

Theme connection: Lies

Age suitability: 11+

Resources needed: A table, a coin

Venue requirements: A room with a table long enough to seat two teams facing each other

Background preparation: You'll need a group of more than four young people to make this work

The game

Divide your group into two teams, and seat them facing each other over the table (or other suitable hard surface). Give one side a coin and instruct them to pass it secretly between themselves below the surface of the table so the opposing team can't see.

At a certain point the opposing team calls "Up Jenkins", at which point all the members of the first team have to clench their fists, secretly grasping the coin if it is in their possession at that point, and place both elbows on the top of the table with their hands clenched above them. The opposition then call "Down Jenkins", at which point every player on the first team has to slam their hands down onto the table palms down and hold them there.

The person with the coin in their hand has to get it under the palm of their hand without the opposition seeing or hearing it, because the aim of this game is for the opposition to identify where the coin is. To do this, the opposition need to eliminate hands one at a time, by agreeing as a team which hand to nominate. Each hand is then lifted, revealing (or not) the coin, with the aim on the part of the guessing team to leave the hand with the coin under it till last.

They therefore keep going either until the coin is revealed, or until there is only one hand left (hopefully concealing the coin). If the coin is revealed before this, the team with the coin wins the point. If the guessing team correctly leave the coin-concealing hand till the end then they win the point. At the end of the round the teams swap roles. Play a number of rounds to identify the winning team. Once the group has "got" how the game works, expect all kinds of mind games and intrigues to develop spontaneously as players try to persuade the opposition that a coin is/isn't hidden under a particular hand…

What's the purpose?

Possible learning/discussion points from this game:

- Is it easier to convince the opposition that your hand has a coin under it when it doesn't, or that it doesn't have the coin under it when it does? Why?

- Is a lie of omission better than any other kind of lie?

- Is there such a thing as a "white lie"? Are they OK?

164. Help my Neighbour

Theme connection: Community

Age suitability: 9+

Resources needed: A pair of dice, several packs of playing cards (one per four players)

Venue requirements: Tables, or flat surface to play on

Background preparation: None

The game

Give each player a set of cards, numbering from two up to the queen, and get them to lay them out sequentially face-up in front of them. The first player rolls the dice, and adds up the total score displayed, turning over their correspondingly numbered card (eleven is the jack, twelve is the queen).

They then have another roll, and turn over the corresponding card to the new total, etc. If they roll a number of a card they have already turned face down, however, their turn is over, unless one of their neighbours either side of them still has that card face up, in which case they can flip that card face down and continue their turn.

Their turn finishes when after a roll of the dice they can no longer turn over their relevantly numbered card, or the cards of either of their neighbours. The dice then pass to the next player, and play continues in exactly the same way. The winner is the first player to turn all their cards face down.

What's the purpose?

Possible learning/discussion points from this game:

- How did you feel about helping your neighbour in this game?

- How do you feel about doing so in real life?

- Jesus was asked "Who is my neighbour?"; what was/is his answer?

165. Blink balloon debate

Theme connection: Value, judgement

Age suitability: 14+

Resources needed: Job titles (on slips of paper)

Venue requirements: None

Background preparation: Prepare enough pieces of paper with job titles on for each member of the group to have one. Before you start the game, make sure you know how many are in your group, and how many of them make up one third.

The game

As they arrive, give everyone a piece of paper with a job title on it. The jobs should be very varied in terms of their perceived 'worthiness'; ranging from things like "Surgeon General" to "Drug Dealer." Ask them to think about why this person's role is needed in society; to consider all the positive contributions they make.

Once everyone has arrived, explain that you are all passengers on a fictional hot air balloon. The balloon is losing altitude, and the only way to save the majority is to throw a third of you overboard! This is a classic philosophical exercise called the balloon debate, but you're going to play a short-attention-span version: everyone has twenty seconds to explain to the group why they should live!

At the end of that time, the group takes a vote as to whether the person gets to live or die. Once everyone has spoken, check whether you've managed to eliminate a third of the group. If not, repeat the exercise with the survivors – but this time they only have ten seconds to explain why they should make the cut.

What's the purpose?

Possible learning/discussion point from this game:

- We make snap decisions on people – often judging them and making lots of assumptions about them within just a few seconds of meeting. Thankfully, that's not how God judges us.

166. Spoons (cards)

Theme connection: Justice, greed

Age suitability: 11+

Resources needed: Enough spoons for one per player, less one, a full pack of playing cards

Venue requirements: None

Background preparation: Set aside from the pack of cards as many sets of equally valued cards (e.g. four aces, four twos, four kings) as there are players

The game

Get your players seated in a circle, ideally around a table, or failing that an open space on the floor that is equally accessible to each player. In the middle of the table (or floor) place as many spoons as there are players, minus one.

Take all the sets of four cards, combine and shuffle well, and then deal them out, four per player. When everyone has their cards, to start the game you as leader simply say "pass": at which point each player selects one of their cards and passes it to the player on their left. You then continue by repeating this passing process until someone achieves the goal of collecting a set of four cards of the same value (it doesn't matter the value of the card, as long as all four are the same).

As soon as someone does so, they simply pick up one of the spoons. At this point everyone else needs to grab for a spoon in an effort not to be the only person left without a spoon.

Whoever it is who is left spoonless is told a letter in the sequence S-P-O-O-N. Once the letter has been allocated, replace the spoons and gather up the cards, shuffle and deal out again, and repeat the whole process. Once a player has been given all five letters they are eliminated, and a spoon and set of cards are removed from the game.

(If any player picks up a spoon when no one has a set of four identical cards they receive a letter. Bluffing is allowed, and a fake grab for a spoon – without actually touching them – can cause other players to fall for it, and grab one themselves.)

If time allows, keep repeating until you find a winner.

What's the purpose?

Possible learning/discussion point from this game:

- This game relies on there not being enough of something to go round equally – you could use this to open up a discussion on whether there are enough resources to go round, or to talk about sharing, greed, etc.

167. If you love me, baby, smile

Theme connection: Evangelism

Age suitability: 9+

Resources needed: None

Venue requirements: None

Background preparation: None

The game

Get your group sitting in a circle and explain that communicating with each other is important, as is love, and that you want your group to love each other. Explain that the first person needs to turn to the person on their right and tell them, with a completely straight face,

"If you love me, baby, smile", at which point that person has to reply, without smiling or laughing (or anything like that), "I love you, baby, but I just can't smile".

If they manage this then they pass it on to the person on their right, "If you love me, baby, smile", etc... If they fail, however, and start laughing/smiling then they are eliminated, and the person who is saying it to them then has to say it to the next person in the circle who again has to keep a completely straight face and reply, etc.

Explain that your group are absolutely allowed, even encouraged, to try to make the people who they are speaking to laugh, by means of funny faces/voices, etc. – as long as they themselves don't smile or laugh while doing so.

Keep it going around the circle until you find the most emotionless automatons/self-controlled people in your group.

What's the purpose?

Possible learning/discussion points from this game:

- The word we translate as gospel comes from the Greek word euangelion which literally means "good news" – in fact it is the best news, the most exciting and important news that humanity has ever received. God loves us, and showed it by sending Jesus, who conquered death and sin for us. If you love this news, baby, then smiling is the least of the responses that we can ultimately offer...

- Have a discussion what kinds of responses the group has received when talking about Jesus.

168. Flour cutting

Theme connection: Consumerism

Age suitability: 7+

Resources needed: Flour, dessert bowls, plates/trays, Smarties, table knife

Venue requirements: None

Background preparation: To prepare for this game you will need a big bag of flour, as well as a dessert bowl into which you carefully compress as much flour as needed. It is important that you get it tightly packed into the bowl, because the next step is to (carefully!) turn it out onto a plate or tray. It can help if you refrigerate it for a couple of hours before turning it out, and it may be worth having a couple in reserve in case the turn-out process doesn't end up as successful as hoped! Once you're ready to turn it out, place the plate/tray over the bowl and then turn it over. Once you have done so successfully, carefully place a small sweet such as a Smartie onto the top of the mound.

The game

Get your group around the mound of flour, and get the young people to take turns to use a simple table knife to carefully slice and remove a section of the flour mound, continuing until the sweet is eventually dislodged. When this happens, the individual who dislodged the sweet has to remove it from the flour, using only their mouth.

This works best with smaller groups, so if you have more than about eight players around a plate, consider using a second bowl and playing off as teams against each other, counting up the highest number of "cuts" made without causing a flour avalanche.

Due to the risk of flour mountains collapsing when the bowl is removed, or when they are moved, you might want to prepare a spare for back-up.

What's the purpose?

Possible learning/discussion points from this game:

- When did you last spend time thinking about what unnecessary rubbish is in your life? How could you remove some of this?

- Is the idea of "simplicity" more likely to fill you with panic or excitement?

169. Beetle Drive

Theme connection: Creation

Age suitability: 9+

Resources needed: Paper and pencil for each player, a dice for every two players

Venue requirements: None

Background preparation: Set up tables around the room in a circle, with a pair of chairs facing each other. Optional: you could draw a basic beetle shape (as the game demands rather than being accurate biologically!) to use as a template or reference for the players during the game. You could also print out a copy of the list of numbers/corresponding body parts to give each player as a reminder

The game

Get your players paired off, and seated opposite each other at each table around the room. Give each player a pencil and piece of paper, and give each pair a dice. Explain that the point of the game is to be the first person to complete drawing a beetle.

Taking it in turns the players roll the dice, and depending on what number lands face up, the player can then draw the corresponding piece of the beetle. However, they can only draw bits of the beetle onto bits that already exist, so they have to draw a body before they can draw anything else, and they have to draw a head before they can add eyes or antenna. They can only draw one body part per turn.

A completed beetle must have a body (six), a head (five), two wings (four), six legs (three), two antennae (two), and two eyes (one). If a player rolls a body part that is already completed then the game just continues to the opponent's turn. Once a player has completed a beetle, by rolling and drawing all the appropriate body parts, they shout out "Beetle", at which point all the pairs stop rolling and drawing, and add up the number of body parts they have each completed. Once they have done so the winners (highest scorer per pair) move one table clockwise, while the losers move one table anti-clockwise. Repeat until you all hate the *Coleoptera* order of insects, or until one player hits a previously agreed total of beetles drawn.

What's the purpose?

Possible learning/discussion points from this game:

- This could lead into an opportunity to spend some time reflecting on the amazing wonder of God's creation – or a discussion on why nature can seem so beautiful.

- Are some creatures in creation worth more than others? Why? Is humanity at the top of the pile?

170. Skills challenge

Theme connection: Skill, overcoming challenges

Age suitability: 7+

Resources needed: Foam football(s), a number of containers of different sizes, tape

Venue requirements: Space to kick footballs around in

Background preparation: Mark a line from behind which your players will kick the balls at the targets, and using a number of containers of differing sizes (e.g. a small paddling pool, bucket, washing up bowl, mixing bowl) secure them to the ground (e.g. tape the mixing bowl down, so that a ball being chipped into it won't make it topple over), making sure that they are spread out with a couple of feet between each target, and with the larger (and therefore easier) targets closer to the kicking point. Label each target with the number of points available (five for the easiest, up to fifty for the mixing bowl, etc.)

The game

The simple premise of this game is for the players to score points by kicking the football into particular containers – the smaller the container, the more points they score. You will want to divide your group into teams – trying as much as possible to mix up the skill levels and competitiveness – and get the teams to take it in turns to try to kick a (foam) football into one of the targets. Make sure that each player has an equal number of turns, four or five ideally, but depending on how big your group is, make sure you don't have lots of people just standing round doing nothing.

Keep a track of the scores as you proceed, and let the final few competitors know what they need to score to win.

What's the purpose?

Possible learning/discussion points from this game:

- Setting and achieving targets – how does this make you feel?

- Would you rather try and fail, or never try and not be disappointed?

171. Human Shazam

Theme connection: Music, identity

Age suitability: 11+

Resources needed: Some form of music player and speakers

Venue requirements: None

Background preparation: Prepare a soundtrack of some of your favourite music (or your group's – depending on how bad you feel their taste is/how important you feel it is to educate them "musically")

The game

Divide your group into teams and get them to sit together in their teams. Then, taking your ready prepared playlist, play them some music (or however you choose to describe their musical taste!). Ideally (if possible) start the tracks in an obscure section of the song – but let the track keep playing until one of the teams can correctly identify the track title and the artist.

Get the groups to stand up as soon as they think they have an answer, at which point pause the music and ask them for their answer. If they are incorrect, they have to sit down and cannot offer another answer for that track until another team has suggested a wrong answer. If they are correct, then award them some points depending on how long you've played the track for. You could offer twenty-five points if they answer within five seconds, twenty points if within ten seconds, fifteen points if within fifteen seconds, ten points if within twenty-five seconds, and simply five if they get it after that.

Keep track of the scores, and announce the winning team at the end.

What's the purpose?

Possible learning/discussion points from this game:

- You could use this as an opportunity for the group to share their musical favourites with each other, and recognize the diversity of our tastes.

- "Music is brilliant and essential to human well-being" – discuss.

11

Seasonal Games

Merry Christmas! / Happy Easter! / Pentecost Salutations! (delete as appropriate)

Or depending on your church – Suitably appropriate sombreness of Lent/Joyous uprising of Ascension-tide/ Baffled bemusement of Septuagesima, etc, I have more if you want them?

We're going to assume that if you've turned to this chapter, it's because you're currently planning for a festive-themed youth group session. And if so, you've come to the right place. On the following pages you'll find games more Christmassy than an eggnog latte; more Eastery (definitely not a word) than a chocolate bunny.

And more wintery than a snowman tobogganing through the white witch's Narnia; more summery than the taste of suncream in your picnic sandwiches... Because these games also include all those things that you can only do on those one day a year occasions when the weather provides a suitable opportunity for those outdoorsy pursuits that involve sun/warmth/ snow, etc. Or that you can do anytime if you live somewhere with an actual predictable and settled climate, i.e. you don't live in the UK.

Anyway, we figure that at least a few times a year, you'll feel a bit festive – and these games are designed to help you to create that perfect seasonal atmosphere. Although, let's be honest, they're all Christmas and Easter-based. If you want games specifically oriented around the fourth Sunday after Pentecost, you'll need to buy our follow-up book, "Games with Very Little Purpose".

172. Human donkeys

Theme connection: Easter or Christmas (see what we did there?), community, Bible

Age suitability: 11+

Resources needed: Black bin bags, sticky tape, newspapers

Venue requirements: Space to spread out, plus space for a safe race if you choose to have one

Background preparation: Obviously, ensure that your group are aware of the inadvisability of placing a plastic bag over the head as part of their costume

The game

Donkeys, perhaps the most humble and pathetic of animals, played a central role in Jesus' life. He was carried on one – or so the children's carol will have us believe – while he was still in Mary's womb. And it was on another little donkey (or maybe a colt, but who's counting?) that Jesus rode into Jerusalem at the start of what we now call Holy Week. This game pays homage to the little donkey, and to all small horses, everywhere.

Split into teams of four or five, and hand out the black bags, sticky tape, and newspapers. Explain that the aim of this game is to create the best "donkey" in five minutes. The donkey can consist of one or two team members (think pantomime horse), plus a costume made out of these simple resources. After five minutes, you'll ask your "donkeys" to walk from one end of your venue to the other – the designs should be judged on both artistic merit and ability to hold together. Award a small prize to the team with the best donkey.

If you want to extend the activity (and the costumes look robust enough), why not culminate with a (safe) "donkey derby" race? You may want to find a way of securing the two team members together in each "donkey" if you attempt this.

What's the purpose?

Possible learning/discussion points from this game:

- A fun way to introduce sessions involving Bible stories that feature a donkey element (see also: Balaam's talking ass).

- Amos 3:3 asks "Do two walk together unless they have agreed to do so?" – harmony between two people is only possible when we both make an effort to walk in the same direction.

- This game could help you to explore further the Christmas or Easter story, using donkeys as a springboard!

173. Sprout Roulette

Theme connection: Hidden gifts, grace, Christmas

Age suitability: 9+

Resources needed: Box of chocolate truffles, some Brussels sprouts, some chocolate for melting, cocoa powder, paper, pens, hat (or bag)

Venue requirements: None

Background preparation: To prepare for this game, take a small box of chocolate truffles and remove a couple of them. (Why not reward yourself at this stage for your wonderful work over the course of the year by eating the ones you remove?) Next, take a couple of sprouts, lightly boil them, and allow to cool (and dry) before dipping them into some melted chocolate. (You may want to double dip to make sure any imperfections in the first layer of covering are covered.) Lightly dust the finished product with some cocoa powder, and voilà, chocolate sprouts, that look uncannily like chocolate truffles. In fact, if you've done it well, they should be virtually indistinguishable from genuine confectionery.

(If your skills as a chocolatier are slight, you could substitute Ferrero Rocher, carefully unwrapping a couple of the aforementioned treats that an ambassador might share, and rewrapping your sprout surprises in the original wrapper, again so they are indistinguishable from the genuine chocolates.) Now number each "chocolate" in the box and place pieces of paper with each number on folded up into a bag or hat. If your group is larger than the number of chocolates you have, then pad it out with some blank pieces of paper, ensuring there are enough for each young person to have a piece of paper. As always with food-based games, check allergies and tailor the game accordingly. Also be sensitive to any young people with issues around food

The game

Pass the bag/hat around and get each young person to take out a piece of paper. Reveal to them that this number represents their prize and corresponds to a chocolate in your prize box. Add almost as an afterthought that a number of the chocolates might not be quite what they seem.

Enjoy watching the young people take their chocolate one at a time and bite into it, share their delight as they realize they have a genuine chocolate, and relish their healthiness if they end up with one of their five-a-day...

Sprout roulette can also be adapted to be the "reward" for any game that you play – simply offer a choice of chocolates as the prize to your winners.

What's the purpose?

Possible learning/discussion points from this game:

- Presents are fun. Jesus got presents from the wise men. He may have been disappointed with myrrh and frankincense, as he probably would have preferred a toy train. Link this to the young people's disappointment as they discovered a sprout in their chocolate.

- Is it better to give or to receive? (Answer honestly!)

174. Christmas alphabet game

Theme connection: Christmas, consumerism

Age suitability: 7+

Resources needed: None

Venue requirements: None

Background preparation: None

The game

Sit the group in a circle, and explain that you're going to play a Christmas version of the kids' classic, the Alphabet game – a memory game which involves thinking of objects beginning with each letter of the alphabet, and then remembering the ever increasing list of objects that you're creating together.

The first person should think of something that they would buy at Christmas beginning with the letter "A" (e.g. Angel), then say: "I went to do my Christmas shopping and I bought an [item]…" The second person then repeats this, but adds a second item beginning with "B". This continues as you move around the circle, with the later group members having to remember more and more items. By the time you reach the letter "M", the group are having to remember thirteen items, and so on.

As Christmas shopping can involve buying almost anything, you can be fairly generous on allowable words – but see if the group can struggle all the way to "Z"!

What's the purpose?

Possible learning/discussion point from this game:

- Christmas has become synonymous with buying loads of stuff. Some people save all year for the festive period, while others end up in a lot of debt each January. But Christmas is about much more than buying stuff!

175. Egg Tossing

Theme connection: Overcoming challenges, Easter

Age suitability: 9+

Resources needed: An egg per pair of players, paper towels, paper, sticky tape, glue, cotton wool, string (or other craft materials as appropriate)

Venue requirements: Large open (outdoor) space

Background preparation: Let your young people know in advance that there is potential for mess

The game

This activity can be done with a touch of creativity or as a simple, straightforward, messy game. The simplest way of running it is to pair your young people up, give them an egg each, and get them to stand facing each other (in two lines) and throw their eggs to each other. If the egg breaks or cracks, that pair is out. If the egg survives undamaged, get the pair to move slightly further apart. Eventually (hopefully) you will end up with a pair of competitors hurling an egg huge distances.

If you wanted to make more out of it, give your group twenty minutes before the throwing starts to create something to protect their egg as they throw/catch it. The only rule is that it needs to be easy to open, to allow checking after each throw to see if the egg is damaged. Provide whatever craft supplies you may have to facilitate this.

What's the purpose?

Possible learning/discussion point from this game:

- We can sometimes feel like we're being thrown about in life, with nothing to protect us from damage – but we can trust that Jesus will always catch us safely.

176. Egg Walking

Theme connection: Journeying, sin, Easter

Age suitability: 9+

Resources needed: Large, strong floor covering (ideally a tarpaulin). Lots of eggs, paper towels, bowl of water for washing, blindfolds, stopwatch (optional)

Venue requirements: A space with an open, flat floor

Background preparation: Lay out your tarpaulin on the floor and liberally place eggs all over it (the more the better!)

The game

Blindfold your young people and get them to walk one at a time (no foot-sliding) across the tarpaulin in their bare feet. Ensure there is a bowl of water and towels at the end to wash any egg off feet. If you have a competitive group, why not time the young people as they travel across (ensure they walk – slippery eggs and running are not a good combination) and add ten seconds of time per egg damaged?

However, no matter how much you try to sell the aim of the game as simply being to cross without standing on any eggs, the young people will basically just enjoy walking on and crushing eggs. In between contestants, be ready to step onto the sheet yourself and remove as much broken eggshell as possible to minimize risk to feet, as well as replacing eggs for the next participant to walk on.

What's the purpose?

Possible learning/discussion points from this game:

- Eggs are surprisingly strong, due to the structure of the shell – so much so that it is possible to stand on one without breaking it (although not in this game!). So just like the egg that seems to be weak, but is actually pretty perfectly designed, the Easter narrative tells us of something – Jesus' going to his death on the cross – that seemed to be weak but turns out to be stronger than anything else in history.

- Life is a journey and there are obstacles along the way. Is this how your group think of life?

177. Miracle on 34th Tree, or the Nightmare Before Christmas Tree

Theme connection: Appearance, Christmas

Age suitability: 9+

Resources needed: A pile of Christmas decorations (the gaudier the better). Think tinsel, candy canes, lights, fairies, stars, baubles, and so on!

Venue requirements: None

Background preparation: Divide your decorations into equally sized piles for each group

The game

Divide your group into small groups and present them each with a pile of your decorations – giving them five minutes to turn one of their team into the tackiest possible Christmas tree. (If you want to turn the lights on, think about using battery operated lights rather than mains powered ones, as these can get hot.)

What's the purpose?

Possible learning/discussion point from this game:

- Just as we decorated the tree with tinsel and pointless decorations, so we often dress up our lives with hollow baubles. With Jesus we don't need to do this.

178. Reindeer antlers

Theme connection: Faith, Christmas

Age suitability: 9+

Resources needed: For every three members of your group you will need a pair of tights, and a packet of (uninflated) balloons

Venue requirements: None

Background preparation: None

The game

Divide your group up into small groups of about three. Give each group one pair of tights and a big handful of uninflated balloons. Instruct them that they have five minutes to inflate the balloons, stuff them into the tights, and turn them into the best possible pair of antlers, which one of them then has to wear while you or another leader judges the "best reindeer".

What's the purpose?

Possible learning/discussion point from this game:

- Reindeer have antlers. Rudolph was a reindeer. Rudolph's red nose guided the other reindeer through the sky. Likewise,

Jesus guides us. Or, more seriously, what should we as Christians think about all the "Father Christmas" stuff that gets mixed in with the season?

179. Santa, Reindeer, Elf

Theme connection: Teamwork, Christmas

Age suitability: 11+

Resources needed: None

Venue requirements: None

Background preparation: None

The game

A festive variation of the classic rock, paper, scissors game. Instead of using hand shapes to indicate the choice, this game involves using the whole body to show which element is chosen, and of course has a certain Christmassy vibe.

The three choices are Santa, Reindeer, and Elf, and are indicated as follows. For Santa, puff out your cheeks in the manner of a jolly old man, and shake your sides with your hands as if chortling with Jolly-St-Nick-esque mirth. For the Reindeer, make two extravagant antlers with your arms/hands coming out from your head, and paw the ground with one foot as if preparing to take flight. For the Elf, crouch down as small as possible, and make a hammering motion with your hands as if constructing some sort of wooden toy.

Demonstrate these actions to your group, and explain that Santa beats the Elf (not literally, of course, we assume he's a good boss) because he is his employer. The Elf beats the Reindeer, because the elves look after and feed the reindeer (try not to think too hard about the elaborate fantasy this game requires!) and the Reindeer beats Santa, because if there were no Reindeer to pull the sleigh there would be no way of getting the presents to all the little children. (As per rock, paper, scissors, two matching actions result in a draw, and no one wins.)

Having explained the premise, get your group to pair off and play a best of three series of engagements to find a collection of winners. Get the winners to pair off and do a best of three again, then repeat until you have a final pair – who then compete in front of everyone to find the ultimate Christmas champion.

What's the purpose?

Possible learning/discussion points from this game:

- If these three didn't work together there'd be no gifts in your stockings (allegedly) – is teamwork something that comes naturally?

- Would you tell young children there was no Santa?

180. Predingo!

Theme connection: Prophecy

Age suitability: 14+

Resources needed: Pens, paper, "bingo" sheets (A4 sheets with ten blank boxes on them), small chocolate prizes

Venue requirements: There should be a safe (and if possible fairly soundproof) place outside the venue for your volunteer to wait

Background preparation: None

The game

(If you hate made-up composite words, this game is called "Prediction Bingo".) Choose a confident volunteer who is fairly well-known to most of the group – although this isn't essential. Now explain that this person is going to spend ninety seconds talking about their experience of Christmas Day last year. Don't give them any prompts at all about what they might say, but take them outside your meeting room and give them a couple of minutes to quickly make some notes.

While they're doing that, give out the bingo sheets and explain to the rest of the group that everyone is going to try to guess ten words or phrases which your volunteer might use during their story. They should write one word or phrase in each box on the sheet.

Bring your volunteer back in, and get them to talk for ninety seconds. The rest of the group should mark off any phrases which the volunteer uses – and if they get all ten, they should shout "PREDINGO!" Give a prize to the winner – and to the volunteer for working so hard.

What's the purpose?

Possible learning/discussion points from this game:

- It's very difficult to predict the future. Yet Jesus' time on earth was correctly predicted by many people, in many ways, over many years.

- Prophecy – the God-given insight to see beyond barriers including time – is a gift that God gives to many throughout the Bible, and offers to his people today.

181. Christmas List

Theme connection: Consumerism, greed

Age suitability: 9+

Resources needed: None

Venue requirements: None

Background preparation: None

The game

A good, quick game for playing in a circle. Get your group seated comfortably, and explain that you are going to share your Christmas present list, and the challenge is that you will go round the circle and take turns to suggest something that is on your Christmas list. You will then tell them whether they are correct or not. Explain that they need to try to work out the rule which you are using to decide whether something is on the list or not.

Get them to use the formula "On my Christmas list this year is…" and then suggest something that might be on your list. The secret rule you need to use is that an item is on the list only if the suggestion starts with the letter that the last correct item ended with. So for example, if you begin with, "On my Christmas list this year is a jumper", then the next person would need to say an item beginning with an "R" for it to be on the list. So if they said "… rabbit", then that would be on the list, whereas if they said "… cat", then you would tell them it's not on the list.

Once a person has had their guess, and you've confirmed whether it's on the list or not, the next person has a go. To make it more tricky, it's only the last letter of the last correct item on the list that counts, so if in our example someone guessed "dog", the next person would still have to suggest an item beginning with R for it to be on the list.

Make sure people who've worked out the rule don't shout it out and spoil it for everyone who's still trying to guess. You can keep this going over a number of sessions if you like, as people get frustrated at trying to work out the rule!

What's the purpose?

Possible learning/discussion points from this game:

- Is greed destroying what Christmas is really about?

- Can we be too hard on the non-traditional elements of Christmas? Do things like presents, decorations, and Christmas TV all add valuable elements to the season, or have they become distractions?

182. Mince Pie Carol-Off

Theme connection: Communication, consumption, greed, Christmas

Age suitability: 9+

Resources needed: Many mince pies

Venue requirements: None

Background preparation: As always with food-based games, check allergies/issues with food and tailor the game accordingly

The game

Divide your group into teams of about half a dozen. For each "round" each team has to nominate one team member to consume a mince pie as quickly as possible, and then recite (or sing, or whistle – dependent on the flakiness of your mince pies, and/or the musicality of your group) a verse of a Christmas carol of your choosing. The first person to successfully and clearly do this, without spraying you in half-chewed mincemeat (or choking, do keep an eye), wins a point for their team. Keep going until you run out of Christmas carols (as if), mince pies (more likely), or patience with the fine mist of crumbs and raisins that now decorates your meeting space (most likely).

If you want to make the game more active, place the mince pies on a plate at the opposite end of the room to the teams, and make the competitors come to you or to another leader to sing their Christmas carol verse.

What's the purpose?

Possible learning/discussion points from this game:

- Do Christmas carols communicate clearly the true meaning of Christmas?

- Does the way you celebrate it clearly do so?

183. Sprout Bowling

Theme connection: Christmas, dislikes

Age suitability: 9+

Resources needed: A supply of raw, unprepared sprouts, some hollow chocolate Santas (the small kind you can hang on a Christmas tree, not the large ones, but they do need to be moulded with a flat bottom otherwise they won't stand up on their own)

Venue requirements: A long table

Background preparation: At one end of the table arrange the Santas to stand as closely as possible in ten pin bowling skittle formation

The game

Gather your players at the other end of the table to the Santas. Explain that you are going bowling, and that their task is to roll a sprout along the tabletop to knock over as many Santas as possible.

One at a time, get them to stand behind the end of the table and attempt to roll a sprout along the surface of the table (no throwing!) and knock over the chocolate pins/Santas. If you have a larger group, play this as a team game, adding together the total number of Santas knocked over by the players of each team. If the group is smaller, however, you could play it as a straightforward head-to-head competition.

If you are feeling generous, allow your players to consume any chocolates they successfully bowl over. Alternatively, you could provide a forfeit (a cooked sprout perhaps?) for any players who fail to bowl any Santas over.

What's the purpose?

Possible learning/discussion points from this game:

- Do you like sprouts? Are there other things about Christmas that you don't like?

- Can you understand why some people might find Christmas a difficult time?

184. Pin the nose on Rudolph

Theme connection: Identity, Christmas

Age suitability: 9+

Resources needed: A red pom pom with double-sided tape attached to it (or something else that looks like a "red nose"), a blindfold, a stopwatch

Venue requirements: None

Background preparation: None

The game

Pick one of your eager young people to play "Rudolph" and another to play "the Pinner". Give the Pinner the "red nose" and explain that they have to try to attach it as close as possible to Rudolph's nose whilst blindfolded. Explain to the other volunteer that they are Rudolph and that they will have to travel round the room on all fours to try to evade the Pinner. They get ten seconds of movement time, during which they have to continuously make reindeer noises (be creative!), and after that they have to stay silent and still. The Pinner then gets twenty seconds to find them and attach the nose. (Adapt the time if your playing space is on the smaller side!)

Award points for skill and accuracy and pick a different pair each time. Get the rest of your young people to (silently) encircle the playing space so that Rudolph doesn't stray too far.

What's the purpose?

Possible learning/discussion point from this game:

* Should things that aren't in the Christmas narrative in the Bible be connected to Christmas like this?

185. Carrot Eating competition

Theme connection: Christmas, Bible

Age suitability: 9+

Resources needed: Plenty of carrots, two plates

Venue requirements: None

Background preparation: Peel or wash enough carrots for one per player. Divide them into two equal piles on the two plates. Place them both at one end of your playing area

The game

Divide your group into two even teams, and get your two teams lined up at the other end of the room opposite a plate each. Explain that they are teams of reindeer, and that they need to eat their carrots before they can go anywhere. One at a time, each team member needs to make their way to the plate of carrots, travelling on all fours just like a reindeer, and without using their hands (again just like a reindeer!) they need to eat a carrot before returning to their team and allowing the next team member to take their turn. The winning team is the first one to consume all their carrots and gather as a team in a reindeer-pulling-a-sleigh formation.

The more extravagant groups might want to play this taking on the role of a group of Santas, and eating mince pies rather than carrots. (Again, no hands.)

What's the purpose?

Possible learning/discussion point from this game:

* There are plenty of things about Christmas that aren't found in the biblical accounts (donkeys, reindeer, carrots, etc.) – does this matter?

12

Quick-Fire Games

So, as we come in to land (to borrow a well-worn youth ministry phrase), we return to the distinction raised in chapter two. Whereas there you found games which could be run without any preparation or equipment, here you'll find the rapidest of rapid-fire ideas; games which you can squeeze into even the most tightly packed youth meeting schedule without fear that you'll overrun. Because, frankly, no one wants to field those angry glares from waiting parents.

> *The distinction is subtle (not something that can be said about many things which I have ever contributed to) but think of these as those things in that mental toolkit of games which fit neatly between the hammer of get-set-go games and the drill bit of energizers (where the hammer is the thing in your toolkit that you turn to when you're not sure what else to use, and the drill is the thing you use when you want to make a lot of noise and a bit of mess). As you can tell, DIY is not my main area of gifting.*

There's nothing worse than a youth group session that's too dry. All right, that's not strictly true; war, famine, and the Fantastic Four remake are all demonstrably worse.

> *Also One Direction after Zayn left, and Twiglets (Marmite, on sticks... urrghhh) are too, but don't let me distract from your flow.*

But it's fair to say that a youth group meeting without any fun in it is no youth group meeting at all. Sometimes, though, you're pressed for time. Your seventeen-point exploration of Daniel in the Lions' Den is going to take time, and you've only got five minutes to spare for a really high-impact game to release enough adrenaline to keep them awake through it. If that's where you find yourself today, you've turned to the right place.

Also, maybe cut out at least one of those points in your exploration of Daniel. The number of objects an average human can hold in their short-term or working memory is seven. Also, yes, fun would be good.

186. What's in the bag?

Theme connection: Faith

Age suitability: 7+

Resources needed: A number of household objects which will be familiar to the young people, but which aren't immediately obvious from their shape – possibilities include a pair of jeans, a specific cuddly toy, kitchen utensils. You'll also need some thick pillowcases or other thin but non-transparent bags, and a way to securely tie these

Venue requirements: None

Background preparation: Secure all the objects inside the bags before the session starts, to avoid anyone spotting them

The game

Hold up an object, securely hidden inside a pillowcase or other bag. Can the young people hazard a guess as to what it might be, just by looking at it? Take a few guesses, and unless someone gets it right, choose a volunteer to feel the bag with their hands. Can they now guess what's in there? If not, choose another volunteer; if by the third young person you still don't have a correct answer, open the bag to reveal what's inside, and move on to another object.

This is also a good game to play as young people are arriving for your session. Place the objects around the room, and invite the young people to move around, feeling the bags and trying to work out what's inside, ready for a big reveal when everyone has arrived.

What's the purpose?

Possible learning/discussion point from this game:

- The Bible says that now we see what's really going on in the world "through a glass darkly" – we get part of the bigger picture, but not all of it. We have to have faith that some of the things that don't make sense now will click into place when God reveals all.

187. Knockout Frisbee

Theme connection: Bullying, teamwork

Age suitability: 11+

Resources needed: A Frisbee

Venue requirements: Outside, large space

Background preparation: None

The game

Get everyone standing in a largish circle suitable for throwing the Frisbee around to each other. (You may want to explain the Goldilocks principle to your group here – not too far, not too close, just right...)
Explain the rules as follows:

- If you throw the Frisbee too badly for anyone to catch it – you're out.

- If you drop the Frisbee whilst attempting to catch it – you're out.

- If you don't make a legitimate attempt to catch the Frisbee when it's clearly thrown to you – you're out (let them know some movement of the feet will be necessary).

Basically the rule of thumb is if you can catch it, you need to do so – all without the Frisbee touching the ground. Diving catches, fumbles, and rebounds are all OK as long as the Frisbee remains off the floor! Also forbidden is throwing it to the people standing either side of you (until you only have four players left), which as the game progresses requires keeping careful note of who is out or not.
Other than that the game consists simply of throwing the Frisbee

between the people in the circle and gradually knocking people out (get them to sit down where they are so other players know who is in/out). You may want to impose a rule as to how hard they can throw the Frisbee depending on the nature of your group (!).

A good way to get the group working together is to let "democracy" decide whether a player has made sufficient attempt to catch a Frisbee, or whether the throw was too bad. Encourage honest and unselfish behaviour and this game can become a real demonstration of Christian living. (Equally, if the group becomes too competitive, get together with your leaders and practise till you can confidently beat any of your young people, and then take delight in knocking out the most competitive of your group early on in the game to give others a chance to shine.)

What's the purpose?

Possible learning/discussion points from this game:

- Does this game bring out the best or worst in you?

- Were some people "chosen" by the group to be out first, while others just carried on quietly? Why?

188. Empire

Theme connection: Power, justice

Age suitability: 9+

Resources needed: Paper, pens

Venue requirements: None

Background preparation: None

The game

Give each young person a piece of paper and a pen and get them to write down (secretly) the name of someone famous. Collect the pieces of paper together and read out the list of names. Instruct your group to pay close attention and to try to remember as many as possible.

The way the game works is that the first person has to ask someone else in the group if they were one of the names that you have read out (e.g. Mickey Mouse; someone is *always* Mickey Mouse). So they'd ask "Jonny, were you Mickey Mouse?" If little Jonny did write down Mickey Mouse on their piece of paper, he moves to join the first person's empire, and the first person then gets another go. If, however, Jonny hadn't written down Mickey Mouse, then he gets the chance to grow his empire by picking someone and asking them "Were you so-and-so?" and so on. Continue until one person has accumulated everyone into their empire (or the group have forgotten the names that you read out). If someone who has already accumulated people into their empire is correctly identified as one of the names, then all the people in their empire move across with them to join the new empire. People already identified can give help and advice to their Emperor.

If you have a large group (say thirty plus) then rather than playing the game in the above form which could be rather long and tiresome, divide them into groups of five or six, and get them to work together as an empire from the start, although each of them can still be identified individually and picked off to join a new empire. This introduces an element of strategy, as the decision whether to reveal your name to your teammates at the start can have a crucial impact later in the game.

What's the purpose?

Possible learning/discussion points from this game:

- Empire or Kingdom? What's better? And which do you naturally tend towards?

- Power dynamics often mean the strong get stronger. Is this right or fair?

189. Hurrggh!

Theme connection: Accusation

Age suitability: 9+

Resources needed: None

Venue requirements: None

Background preparation: None

The game

Get everybody standing in a circle, and start the game off by placing your hands together and extending your arms to point at someone while saying loudly and clearly "Hurrgggh". That person then has to place their hands together and extend their arms up above their head, saying (loudly and clearly) "Hurrgggh". Immediately after this, the people each side of them place their hands together and extend their arms diagonally in towards the person in the middle (creating a pyramid-vibe) while simultaneously saying "Hurrgggh". The person in the middle then points with their hands together at someone else in the circle and shouts "Hurrgggh". That person, and their two neighbours, then follow the same routine and so on ad infinitum...

Once everyone has got how the game works, start to eliminate people if they fail to point correctly, don't shout "Hurrgggh" sufficiently enthusiastically, do it at the wrong time, are too slow, break down in laughter, etc. As people are eliminated, get them to sit down so that people need to keep track of who they are now standing next to. You will only be able to play to a final two (it does work with just three players, albeit in a slightly head-meltingly intense way) so either have a pair of winners, or use an alternative activity to decide an ultimate winner. Start playing at quite a slow rhythm initially, but as your group get used to it, speed it up – eventually it will sound like you're all part of a Kung Fu movie!

What's the purpose?

Possible learning/discussion points from this game:

- You can think of the actions of this game as accusing each other, and being supported by your neighbours in that accusation. Does this change the way you look upon the game?

- Have you ever been accused of anything publicly? How did it feel?

190. Knife, fork, spoon

Theme connection: Appearance, God's plan, suffering

Age suitability: 9+

Resources needed: A knife, a fork, and a spoon

Venue requirements: None

Background preparation: Prepare your accomplice as to your secret (copy the posture of the person picked). More will become clear as you read the description below!

The game

Get everyone seated in a circle (including yourself) and place a knife, fork, and spoon in the centre of the circle. Explain to the group that you are going to send one of the other leaders out of the room. While they are gone, you will pick someone in the circle and, upon the leader's return, they will somehow know who that person is.

Demonstrate this by sending your accomplice out, picking someone, and then arranging the knife, fork, and spoon in some form of pattern. Call your accomplice back and watch in amazement as they pick exactly the right person. Offer the chance to any of the group to see if they can work out how this is done, by giving them the opportunity to be the person sent out of the room. Pick someone as before, arrange your cutlery, and upon welcoming back your volunteer see if they can identify who you picked... and repeat.

The twist is, of course, that the arrangement of the cutlery has nothing to do with how your accomplice knows who you picked. Simply secretly instruct them beforehand that you will exactly copy the posture of the person you picked. The group will come up with all kinds of fantastic theories as to how this works, and the more ostentatiously you arrange the knife/fork/spoon, the more outlandish theories they will invent.

Once some of the kids have worked it out, make sure they don't give the game away, and play until the frustration reaches epic proportions. However, don't allow the game to progress to the stage where only a few people haven't worked it out and are left feeling stupid.

What's the purpose?

Possible learning/discussion point from this game:

- This game shows that sometimes there's much more going on, beyond simply what we can see. How tuned-in are we to this idea?

- Sometimes things happen which don't immediately make sense – and can even feel very painful. How do you feel about/ process this?

191. Kingball

Theme connection: Sin, spiritual attack

Age suitability: 9+

Resources needed: A couple of foam footballs

Venue requirements: Enough space for your group to stand in a circle

Background preparation: None

The game

Get your group to stand with feet spread out about shoulder width apart, and touching the feet of the people either side of them, forming an unbroken circle. Get them to place one hand behind their back and explain that with the other hand their task is to prevent the ball from passing between their legs, while simultaneously trying to get it to go through everyone else's legs. The rules are simply that their legs mustn't move, and that they aren't allowed to grab and throw the ball, just hit it.

Once the group has got hold of the dynamics of the game, explain that if the ball does go through a player's legs they are out of the game. (If your group is smaller then have a three life system to prolong participation.)

Once someone is out, get them to sit cross-legged where they'd stood to remain as a barrier, and explain that their job is now to keep the ball in play and to get as many people out as quickly as possible from their seated position. Keep playing until you have a winner.

Tip: This game works well with multiple balls (a ratio of about one ball per seven participants is good; and biblical!) but introduce them one at a time, as your group gets better at the game. Make sure you have helpers standing around outside the circle to quickly return any errant balls to the playing area.

What's the purpose?

Possible learning/discussion point from this game:

- "Extinguish all the flaming arrows of the evil one" (Ephesians 6:16) – what does this mean? Do your group ever think about this and how to do it?

192. Bodyguard

Theme connection: Sacrifice, heroism

Age suitability: 9+

Resources needed: A foam football (or two)

Venue requirements: Enough space for your group to stand in a large circle

Background preparation: None

The game

Get the group standing spread out in a large circle and choose two players to stand in the middle. Nominate one of them as the Target and the other as their Bodyguard. Explain that they are both free to move around anywhere within the circle (but not out of it), and that the Bodyguard's job is to prevent the Target from being hit by the ball (therefore to put their body between them and the ball). Everyone else's job is to try to hit the Target by throwing the ball at them.

The Bodyguard is counted as invulnerable, but once the Target is hit directly (disallow rebounds, or indirect touches) they are "out" and return to the circle, while the Bodyguard becomes the new Target, and the person who threw the ball that hit the Target becomes their new Bodyguard. Tell your group that this change happens immediately and that any new Target/Bodyguard needs to move quickly to avoid any hit occurring before they can get into place.

To begin, give a ball to someone standing in the circle and

announce open-season on the Target! Keep playing until you get a pairing in the middle who work so efficiently that no one can get them; at this stage you could introduce a second ball if the circle is large enough.

Tip: You will need to ensure the circle doesn't gradually get smaller as the group edges inwards towards the pair in the middle. Suggest that they pass the ball around the circle rather than just throwing the ball directly at the Target.

What's the purpose?

Possible learning/discussion points from this game:

- Sacrificing yourself for someone else – would you ever do this?

- Do people think of Jesus more as a teacher, an inspirational figure, or as a sacrifice for sin? Can these be truly separated? Which is easier to think about?

193. Glove racing

Theme connection: Pressure, stress

Age suitability: 9+

Resources needed: Two pairs of gloves

Venue requirements: None

Background preparation: None

The game

Get your group seated in a circle. Space out your gloves individually and evenly around the circle, and explain that the aim of the game is to manage to put on, and take off, a glove and pass it on to the next person in the circle before the next glove catches up. Anyone who ends up holding both gloves at the same time is out, and the glove skips them in the future as it continues round the circle.

Keep eliminating players until it becomes untenable to continue, or until you find 2 people who are really adroit at putting on and removing gloves quickly. The best gloves for this game are small rubber gloves that are tricky to easily slip on or off. Allow for one glove every 4 people or so to make the game tense and busy. Keep a close eye on the game and whenever a player is caught in a two-glove pile-up, make everyone else pause in the putting on/removal of the gloves, and space them out evenly again before continuing.

If your group are good enough at the game to continue, remove a glove from the circle when there begins to be too many gloves for the numbers.

What's the purpose?

Possible learning/discussion points from this game:

- How do you cope under pressure?

- What are things which get you stressed? Exams? Parents? Friendships? Appearance? What do you do to survive stress?

194. Scatterball

Theme connection: Teamwork, identity

Age suitability: 9+

Resources needed: A foam ball

Venue requirements: A hall with a high(ish) ceiling

Background preparation: None

The game

Get everybody in the centre of your hall touching the ball (or as close to it as you can get dependent on numbers!) – count down three, two, one and throw the ball up into the air. At this stage anyone can then grab the ball and throw it at anyone else, with the usual dodgeball rule that if the ball hits you on the legs then you are "out".

In this variation, anyone who is out sits down on the floor where they've been hit. They can, however, still participate in the game and throw the ball at people to try to get them out, but cannot move from where they are sitting. Players who are not out yet are at liberty to move around the playing area as they wish. However, if they pick up the ball to throw it at someone, they are only allowed to take one step while holding the ball. The game is played until there is only one player left in. Repeat until group is exhausted, or runs out of desire to play. (This won't happen, by the way.)

What's the purpose?

Possible learning/discussion points from this game:

- Individuality or teamwork? Which is your preference?

- How do different types of people respond to the scattering at the start of each round? Why might people react differently?

195. The toilet roll game

Theme connection: Communication, community, identity

Age suitability: 11+

Resources needed: Lots of toilet roll!

Venue requirements: None

Background preparation: None

The game

Get the group into a circle, and put all the toilet rolls in the middle. Now tell everyone in the group to go and take "as much toilet paper as you think you need". Don't say any more than that – in fact be deliberately cryptic, simply repeating that phrase again in response to any questions. Eventually everyone should begin to take some paper – don't put any restriction on how much they take.

Once everyone is back and seated in their original position, reveal the twist: each person now has to tell the group some facts about themselves... and they have to give you one fact for each sheet of toilet roll that they've taken.

There will be some people who've just taken a single sheet, and others who've taken just two or three. Get them to speak first, leaving you with... the inevitable one or two people who have taken near enough a whole roll. If you're pushed for time, be merciful and cut them short at ten or so facts – but if time allows and the facts keep coming, then let them talk...!

What's the purpose?

Possible learning/discussion point from this game:

- Sometimes we can find it difficult to build strong, lasting relationships – but one of the keys to successful friendship is communication. This game allows lots of new conversations to begin within your group – make sure you follow up on any hidden talents, interests, or even pastoral issues that are raised by the lists of facts you hear.

196. Newspaper Square

Theme connection: Putting burdens onto others

Age suitability: 9+

Resources needed: A large square of paper (or folded tarpaulin or sheet)

Venue requirements: None

Background preparation: None

The game

Place your large square of paper in the middle of the room. Get your players to stand around it in a circle holding hands, and explain that they are not allowed to step onto the paper. If they do they are out. Inevitably, once you inform them of this and start the game, they will twig that they can try and pull each other onto the paper. As people are pulled onto it, eliminate them from the circle, and reset everyone so that the paper is in the centre once more before beginning again.

As the circle gets smaller, you may need to reduce the size of the square, but ensure it's still big enough that it's not easy to simply step over. (As a general rule of thumb, as long as the "square" is around one square metre, this is a good size. If you're using newspaper sheets, make sure you have spares as they get ripped easily when involuntarily trod on!) This is a game to be careful with – if your group is particularly "physical" or unevenly matched in size, you may want to take particular care.

What's the purpose?

Possible learning/discussion point from this game:

- Causing problems for other people (aka trying to pull them onto the paper) seems fun. Why might it not be a good strategy in life?

197. The Key Game

Theme connection: Hearing, vision, Bible

Age suitability: 9+

Resources needed: Large and jangly bunch of keys, blindfold or torch (dependent on variation of game), a chair

Venue requirements: None

Background preparation: Set one chair in the middle of the room and place the keys underneath it

The game

Get everybody seated in a large circle around a chair in the centre of the room. Under the chair place a large and jangly bunch of keys, and position somebody on the chair. Blindfold them, and explain that the aim of the game is for another player (secretly nominated by you, the leader) to sneak up on the person on the chair and steal their keys, and that the person on the chair has to catch them by pointing at them.

To make it harder the person on the chair can only make three points (and is not allowed to make a sweeping gesture – defined points only!). If any part of the key-thief is pointed at, they lose, and return to their original seat while you pick a new "thief". If the thief is successful at evading detection, however, they get to be the person on the chair.

If your playing area can be dark enough (and it does need to be really dark), you can play a variant where instead of blindfolding the person on the chair, simply equip them with a focused torch (think Maglite, or any form of torch where the beam can be focused to a very specific point). To make it harder, the person on the chair can only use the torch once, and not sweep it round. However, if any part of the key-thief is illuminated by the torch beam, they lose. If the thief is successful at evading detection, they get to be the person on the chair.

Tip: This variation only works when it is properly dark, so make sure any windows into the room are covered and any fire-escape lights are (temporarily!) covered. For the other two games above, the darker the better, but complete pitch-blackness isn't required.

What's the purpose?

Possible learning/discussion points from this game:

- Have any of your group had any experience of losing one of their senses (even temporarily)? If so, what was it like?

- "The light shines in the darkness, and the darkness has not overcome it" (John 1:5); what do your group make of this Bible verse?

198. Actual Consequences

Theme connection: Narrative, identity, community

Age suitability: 9+

Resources needed: Paper, pens, five pots/boxes which are labelled: When, Where, Who, What Happened First, and What Happened Next

Venue requirements: None

Background preparation: Set out the five pots, and put piles of paper and pens next to each

The game

Instruct your group to think back over their past year and to highlight one exciting/interesting/funny thing that happened to them or their loved ones. They then need to write down the appropriate part of the story on the bits of paper next to each pot, and fold up that piece of paper and put it into the relevant pot. Explain that they have to be actual things that happened, although they are allowed to make up fictitious pen names for the "Who" pot.

Then draw out a piece of paper from each pot and seamlessly weave them together as a story – allow people to try to guess who the different bits of the story were from before revealing the authors.

What's the purpose?

Possible learning/discussion point from this game:

- Stories are a key element of who people are, and a great way of getting to know somebody. Do we spend enough time listening to each other's stories? Did your group find it easy to recognize each other's stories?

199. Blind Square

Theme connection: Communication, listening to God

Age suitability: 11+

Resources needed: A long cord/rope (long enough for all the group to hold onto, whilst comfortably spaced apart) and enough blindfolds for each member to be blindfolded. A physical representation of a shape

Venue requirements: None

Background preparation: None

The game

Get your group into a circle, holding onto the rope, and blindfold them. Explain that you are going to give them a shape which they need to form themselves into (e.g. square, triangle, circle, etc.).

Once they have managed to do this, get them to organize themselves into particular shapes as instructed, but this time without speaking. For another variant of the challenge, don't simply tell the group what the shape is, but give one member of the group (still blindfolded) a model of the shape and get them to communicate to the rest of the group what they can feel.

What's the purpose?

Possible learning/discussion points from this game:

- How can we communicate if we can't speak? How do we pass on our messages?

- How does God speak to us? Mostly we don't hear an audible voice, so how else do we hear him?

200. Wink Chair Grab

Theme connection: Communication, holding onto things

Age suitability: 9+

Resources needed: Chairs for half your group

Venue requirements: Enough room for a circle of chairs and people to stand behind them

Background preparation: None

The game

Get half of your group sitting in a circle on chairs, and the other half standing behind them, so that each chair, apart from one, has someone sitting on it and someone standing behind them. You will also need one person to stand behind the empty chair, and their task is to attempt to fill the space in front of them. They do so by subtly winking at someone sitting down, who then has to move to sit in the empty chair.

The person standing behind them has to try to keep them there by touching both shoulders before they can get out of reach. If they succeed, that person stays in their seat and the "winker" has to wink at someone else. If they fail then they become the person with the empty chair and so have to try to get someone to fill it, and so on... After a while swap roles so that the seated people become grabbers and vice versa. Ensure that the grabbers stand with hands by their sides rather than poised menacingly by the shoulders of the person seated in front of them. Emphasize that they only need to touch, NOT HIT or GRAB, the person on their chair to keep them in place!

What's the purpose?

Possible learning/discussion points from this game:

- Change can be scary and we like to hold on to keep things the way they were. Discuss.

- Were players looking to catch the eye of the "winker" or to make life easier by avoiding it? How does that relate to the way we might approach everyday life?

Index of Themes

Also from Monarch Books:

The Ideas Factory *Martin Saunders*

100 ADAPTABLE DISCUSSION STARTERS TO GET TEENS
TALKING

ISBN: 978-0-85721-680-9

The Ideas Factory is a priceless PHOTOCOPIABLE
resource for youth leaders.

The 100 discussion starters contain a story followed
by questions picking up on key themes or ideas. Each
explores a topic pertinent to young people, such as
drugs, truancy, or parental relationships; or an important
biblical concept, such as giving, the afterlife, or love. The
questions begin with general issues, before moving on to
what the Bible has to say.

The last 25 discussion starters provide a journey through the main stories and
themes of the Bible.

The Think Tank *Martin Saunders*

100 ADAPTABLE DISCUSSION STARTERS TO GET
TEENS TALKING

ISBN: 978-0-85721-681-6

This book contains 100 FREE TO PHOTOCOPY stories
designed to provoke discussion, followed by penetrating
questions which relate the stories to biblical bedrock.

The stories are in four parts:

- **WOULD YOU BELIEVE IT?** – Unbelievable stories,
  all absolutely true!

- **INSPIRING INDIVIDUALS** – Stories of celebrities,
  public figures and other people of note making a positive difference.

- **WHAT WOULD YOU DO?** – Ethics explored through stories, many based on real
  events.

- **TALKING MOVIES** – A major bonus: 25 movie clips that pack a punch with
  young people, and all the background and questions you'll need to facilitate
  discussion around them.

  www.lionhudson.com

Printed and bound by CPI Group (UK) Ltd, Croydon, CR0 4YY

25/03/2025

14647532-0005